Abandoned Places

TONINO GUERRA

ABANDONED PLACES

POEMS

TRANSLATED FROM THE ROMAGNOLE
ITALIAN BY ADRIA BERNARDI

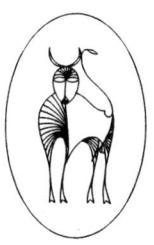

GUERNICA
Toronto·Buffalo·Lancaster (U.K.)
1999

Originally published in Italy as
Il miele, La capanna, Il viaggio,
and *Il libro delle chiese abbandonate.*

Copyright © 1981, 1985, 1986, 1988, 1999, by Tonino Guerra.
Translation © 1999, by Adria Bernardi and Guernica Editions Inc.
All rights reserved.

Antonio D'Alfonso, editor
Guernica Edition Inc.
P.O. Box 117, Station P, Toronto (Ontario), Canada M5S 2S6
2250 Military Rd., Tonawanda, N.Y. 14150-6000 U.S.A.
Gazelle, Falcon House, Queen Square, Lancaster LA1 1RN U.K.
Typesetting by Faye Martin, Toronto.
Printed in Canada.

The publisher was assisted by the Ministry of Foreign Affairs
(Government of Italy) through the Istituto Italiano di Cultura,
Toronto (Director: Francesca Valente).

Legal Deposit — First Quarter
National Library of Canada.
Library of Congress Catalog Card Number: 95-81893

Canadian Cataloguing in Publication Data
Guerra, Tonino
Abandoned places
(Essential poets series ; 74)
Poems translated from 4 books: Il miele, La capanna, Il viaggio, Il
libro delle chiese abbandonate.
ISBN 1-55071-030-3
1. Guerra, Tonino — Translations into English.
I. Bernardi, Adria, 1957 - II. Title. III. Series.
PQ4867.U3A72   1999   851'.914   C95-920995-6

Contents

Translator's Acknowledgments 6
Introduction by Rebecca West 7

PART ONE

A Trilogy of Return and Departure

I. The Honey 23
II. The Hut 65
III. The Journey 93

PART TWO

The Book of Abandoned Churches

The Valley of White Churches 113
The Cracks 114
The Black Spot 115
The Breakfast 116
The Words Inside a Stone 117
The Sandals 118
Two Coffee Mills 119
The Sheep 120
The Streak 121
The Butterflies 122
A Buttonhole of the New Jacket 123
The Bowing Candles 124
The Bell 125
The Water of the Parish 126
The Big Church 127
The Corner 128
The Cherry Leaves 129
The Graveyard of Rusted Crosses 130
SSSH! 131
The White Horse 132
The Disobedient Hen 133
The Garden of the Nuns 134
The Mulberry 135
The Trench 136
Translator's Note 137

Translator's Acknowledgments

I would like to thank the following people: Annamaria Torriglia, Rebecca Messbarger, Adeodato Nicolai, Jeffrey Stovall, and, most of all, Rebecca West.

These translations are dedicated to my father, who first learned to speak in dialect.

Adria Bernardi

Introduction

When I first met Tonino Guerra at his apartment in Rome in the fall of 1985, I had begun working on a number of contemporary Italian prose writers more or less of his generation (Calvino, Malerba, Manganelli), and the distinguished scholar Maria Corti had urged me to consider Guerra's work as well. She is a personal friend of Guerra, and had in fact already convinced him to give important manuscripts of his poetry and prose to her then newly burgeoning *Fondo* or Institute of Contemporary Italian Literature, which she had founded at the University of Pavia. With characteristic generosity, Corti had called Guerra upon my arrival at her apartment in Milan that fall, told him of my work (and put a very flustered me on the line to *salute* Tonino), and thus introduced me to a whole new world of creative energies and multiple talents embodied in the man known as Tonino.

Before our actual first meeting, I had 'met' something of Guerra, having read his early collections of poetry and a few of his prose works, but I had formed no clear idea of how he might fit into my work on experimental and postneoavant-garde prose narrative. Soon after meeting him face-to-face, as I sat enthralled and slightly overwhelmed in his colorfully cluttered apartment, listening to his inimitable Romagnole accent and his equally inimitable flow of words, I realized that Tonino Guerra did not and does not fit comfortably into any category. He is — and always has been — an artist, a creator of art, an unquenchable creative force that images forth a world of poetry at once deeply human and soaringly transcendent, be it in screenwriting, drawing, painting, writing prose in 'standard' Italian or poetry in Romagnole dialect — or in the material transformations of his beloved birthplace Santarcangelo di Romagna, which he has made into a place of magic and beauty through civic and collaborative activities I shall detail further on.

To have Tonino Guerra fling open the door to his apartment and, with gruff heartiness, welcome you in, is to enter into his unforgettable personal aura; to open one of his books of poetry (or prose) is equally to enter into an aura: that of genuinely transforming art.

Antonio Guerra was born to a poor family in 1920 in the small town of Santarcangelo di Romagna, near Rimini. In a brief autobiographical sketch included in the volume dedicated to him and published by Rimini's Maggioli Publishing House in 1985, Guerra writes that his mother was illiterate, and he was the one eventually to teach her to write. With his unerring ability to paint a full human portrait in a few words, he further writes that his mother's will, written during the War and hidden in her eyeglass case, read: *Lasio tutti i miei beni a mio marito da fare tutto quello che vole* (I leave all my goods to my husband who can do with them whatever he wishes). He adds that at that time his mother owned only a few vases of flowers.

During the Second World War, the family hid out in a hut outside of Santarcangelo; when Tonino's father sent him back to Santarcangelo to feed the abandoned family cat, the young man was captured and deported to a concentration camp in Troisdorf, Germany. There he began to compose poems in Romagnole dialect for the comfort and delectation of his fellow prisoners, many of whom, like him, came from peasant families of the Emilia-Romagna region.

In the autobiographical sketch, Guerra deftly paints yet another unforgettable portrait, this time of his father. Upon Tonino's release from the prison camp, he returned in 1945 to Santarcangelo, one Sunday morning in August. Knowing that his family believed him to be dead, he sat down on the edge of a ditch near the train station and sent someone on ahead to his home in order to prepare the way by letting his parents know that some Italian prisoners were still making their way back from northern Italy and beyond. He then walked from the station to the family home, where his father stood waiting for him on the threshold:

> We had never kissed or shaken hands; we had hardly ever made any signs of acknowledgment one to the other. I stopped several feet in front of him in order not to make him feel ill at ease. My dad looked at me for a long time, chewing over his short Toscano cigar, then he took the unlit cigar out of his mouth and asked me: 'Have you had something to eat?' 'A lot,' I answered.

His father then hurried off toward town; later, as Tonino sat in the little living room of the family home surrounded by relatives and friends, a man arrived carrying a small case. When asked if he was looking for someone, the man replied: 'I'm the barber. Your father told me that I had to come shave you.' Guerra writes: 'I touch my face and I realize that I have a two-day growth of beard.'

These brief anecdotes masterfully evoke the simplicity, strength, and taciturn but deep bonds of the peasant people from whom Tonino Guerra came, and to whom he will return again and again in his art.

In 1946 Guerra published, at his own expense, his first collection of dialect poetry entitled *I scarabócc*

(Scribblings), which was graced with an introduction by the eminent critic Carlo Bo. He also received a degree from the University of Urbino in the same year, and began to teach in an agrarian school in nearby Savignano. In 1952 he moved to Rome, published some short stories in the *Gettoni* series edited by Vittorini, and began his career as a screenwriter.

For the next two decades Guerra worked with many of Italy's most prominent film directors, from Giuseppe De Santis to Antonioni to Rosi to Monicelli and many others. His collaboration with Antonioni was especially intense; he worked with the director on such classics as *L'Avventura* (1959), *L'Eclisse* (1962), *Deserto rosso* (1964), and *Blow Up* (1966), and critics have begun to recognize Guerra's enormous contribution to the poetry and power of these films. Guerra made his one and only trip to the United States in order to work with Antonioni on *Zabriskie Point* (1969), but the stay was brief as the screenwriter was in the midst of an emotional crisis that resulted in a nervous breakdown. It also resulted in a fictional prose work, very *Antonioni-esque* in its portrayal of modern alienation and angst (or should we call Antonioni *Guerra-esque*?), entitled *L'uomo parallelo* (The Parallel Man) and published by Bompiani in 1969.

From the early 1950s to the 1970s (and beyond), the world of cinema took up Guerra's time and energies, and the essential role that his extraordinary talent as a screenwriter and collaborator had in shaping the great season of Italian cinema is now fully recognized. The frenetic and exhausting life demanded by the filmmaking world had taken both a personal and an artistic toll on Guerra, for he essentially loathed living in Rome (and still did when I met him there in 1985) and he had lost the immediate ties with his beloved Romagna that had nourished his poetry.

The early 1970s mark a sort of turning point, for Guerra returned to poetry, publishing *I bu* (The Oxen) in 1972 with Rizzoli. The collection included both the original dialect and standard Italian versions of the poems, and was introduced by the eminent critic Gianfranco Contini, whose scholarly appreciation for the poetry did much to strengthen Guerra's reputation as a 'real poet.' The two worlds of dialect poetry and cinema came together for Guerra in his close collaboration with Fellini on the film *Amarcord*, in which Fellini's Emilian boyhood and Guerra's Romagnole roots intertwine to form an unforgettable portrait of provincial life in the 1920s and 1930s under Fascism.

In spite of his return to poetry, Guerra continued to collaborate on a number of films in the 1970s and 1980s; he worked with the Taviani brothers on *La notte di san Lorenzo* (The Night of the Shooting Stars) and *Kaos*, with Fellini on *E la nave va* (And the Ship Sails On) and *Ginger e Fred*, and with Francesco Rosi on *Cristo si è fermato a Eboli*, *Tre fratelli*, and *Carmen*. Guerra also collaborated closely with the astounding Russian director, Tarkovski, especially on the deeply poetic film *Nostalghia*.

Russia had become more and more a presence in Guerra's life, for he had married a Russian woman (his second marriage), Lora, with whom he often travelled to the Soviet Union, and through whom he established ties with the Russian cinematic, literary, and scholarly world. His novel, *La pioggia tiepida* (1984), evokes one of these magical trips, interweaving historical, personal, and fantastic elements with great force.

By the early 1980s, Guerra was spending more and more time back in Santarcangelo. He had come through a serious health crisis in need of more constant contact with his native world, and the grind of life in Rome was becoming less and less tolerable to him. When I met him in 1985, I asked him why he had not written his prose works in dialect, and he answered that he had to be there, in Romagna, in order to write in his mother tongue. His decision to do just that, to 'go home again', whatever the conditioning factors, has been our as well as his tremendous gain, for the three collections of dialect poetry included in this volume are the result. And what a glorious result. *E' mél* (1981), *La capana* (1985), and *E' viàz* (1986) form a trilogy centered on life both past and present in and around Guerra's birthplace. Yet they are far more than reminiscences or nostalgic revisitations of beloved places and people. They are poems that create an entire universe, at once vividly alive and gradually fading away, a world that lives and can only live in the language of its people, both of which — language and people — are part of an Italy quickly dying out as modernization and standardization eat away at the provincial and dialectal soul of the country.

I shall end my introduction shortly with a few more brief comments on the collections included in this volume, but first I wish to complete this nutshell biography with some words about Guerra's most recent projects. Since 1986, Guerra has been living more or less full-time in Romagna. My second visit to him, in 1989, was in Santarcangelo, where I began the visit by making a tremendous gaffe. I had met up with an American colleague, also a professor of Italian, and I very much wanted her to have the unforgettable experience of meeting Tonino. My memories of our 1985 meeting in Rome were still vivid — and vividly aglow with the rosy light of remembered happy moments. Tonino and Lora had both been warm, welcoming, wonderfully accommodating to a nervous visitor who was not quite sure of how to proceed. Tonino had agreed to let me record our conversation, and he was expansive, touching, funny, and beautifully eloquent in his responses to my tentative questions. (I subsequently incorporated some of the interview into an article I wrote on his work, and I have often played parts of it for my graduate students in seminars on contemporary poetry.) Tonino gave me materials — proofs of *La capanna*, beautiful posters of his artwork, a copy of the Maggioli book dedicated to him, on the flyleaf of which he drew me one of his signature bowls of fruit — and he and Lora gave me a Russian painted wooden box which has ever since graced my living room. He was a bit gruff, a bit 'rough and ready' in his enthusiasm, a bit overwhelming, but I had never felt during those hours that he was anything but generous-spirited and grandly welcoming.

I had subsequently learned during the next few years in writing to him or calling that he was not easy to pin down, he did not answer letters, he did not like to make advance plans for exact visits. Nonetheless, I was determined to take my friend to Santarcangelo, and to arrange the visit for the ease of Tonino.

We agreed on a day, although not on a specific time, and my friend and I (we were traveling from Bologna) settled on what we thought to be the best train (in terms of simplicity): a local that arrived directly to Santarcangelo. It was a real 'local', a train that stopped at every little place imaginable between Bologna and Santarcangelo, but we felt that to arrive in Rimini and to have to call Tonino for a ride to his town would be an enormous imposition.

Imagine our amazement when we arrived at the station in Santarcangelo, called the Guerra residence, and got an agitated Lora at the other end, who told us that Tonino was waiting for us at the Rimini train station, having assumed that naturally we would take the most direct train!

She was beside herself, stuttering out that Tonino would most certainly return in a foul mood, wondering where the hell those 'American girls' had gotten to. To add fuel to the fire, Lora also told us that since Tonino did not drive, he had gotten a relative to take him to Rimini, thus further adding to the bother we had created. With no small sense of trepidation, my friend and I got a cab from the train station and pulled up in the main square where Tonino and Lora had an apartment over the central bar.

Although the 'magic' of the small town was evident in its spacious central piazza and its quiet atmosphere, we were filled with something very close to dread as we rang the doorbell to the Guerra home. Lora answered, but called down that she was coming out so that she and we could go to the bar and wait out Tonino's dark mood, which she was sure would have descended upon him by the time of his return from Rimini. And so we went to the bar, had a coffee, and tried to get a fix on just how bad the damage was from a still agitated Lora (whose Italian worsened perceptibly when she was upset). Sure enough, within fifteen minutes or so, Tonino and his helpful relative pulled up in front of the bar. Without so much as a glance in our direction, he proceeded to climb the stairs to his apartment.

After another fifteen minutes, Lora said that we could give it a try, and so, feeling more like lambs to the slaughter than happy visitors, we climbed the stairs too. Tonino was mad and it showed. As we tried to explain why we had chosen the train we had chosen, he cut us off and began a sort of tirade against American materialism. I truly did not know what to do, and my poor friend by now was convinced that I must have dreamed the 'poetic', 'fantastic', 'wonderful' Tonino I had told her about.

After a few more minutes of angry bluster, however, he began to calm down, to ask my friend about herself, and to look at me with something like a friendly gaze. We ended up walking all over the town with him and Lora, having its many points of interest explained to us, and eating a great meal in a restaurant decorated with traditional Romagnole tile stoves designed and made by young artists of the region (true works of art). Tonino gave my friend and me numbered prints of some of his recent artwork, signing them with warm words of dedication to us.

By the time we left, all was back to normal, and we took away very happy memories and several group photographs of us, Tonino and Lora, and various friends, from which you would never be able to discern the turmoil that had shortly before reigned.

I have told this unforgettable (at least to me and my friend) story because, upon reflection, it revealed a tremendous amount about regional as well as personal pride to us. My friend and I were coming for the first time to Tonino's Italy (and he knew it was the first time for both of us), and he wanted to welcome us at its threshold, Rimini, in appropriately formal and grand style. By having his relative drive him to the 'big' train station there, he was letting us know in no uncertain terms that he considered us important visitors who should be transported in comfort to Santarcangelo. In our desire to simplify things for him by taking the local straight to Santarcangelo, we had ruined his royal welcome of us into Romagna, no matter how good our motives might have been.

My friend and I are convinced to this day that Tonino's 'fury' was actually a sort of wounded pride that had nothing to do with the inconvenience of his futile drive to Rimini. He had planned and orchestrated a wonderful welcome and we, in our 'American' ignorance, had ruined it, taking away his chance to 'open the door' to Romagna in grand style. Had we but known; had he but said, clearly and unequivocally, that we should take such and such train at such and such time to Rimini, we would have been relieved to comply. But Tonino simply did not imagine such impracticality, such stupidity: that we should take a shabby, slow little local train rather than the train to Rimini. He had quite literally 'imagined,' seen in clear images, what our arrival would be like, and we did not play our parts in making that imagined scene come to life.

It may seem that this is a misreading or an overreading of a simple text: 'the man was inconvenienced and was irritated because of it.' But this is not what it was all about, I am convinced. Tonino could not have fussed about arrival plans beforehand, any more than his father could have fussed about his son's return home. That our visit mattered and that Tonino's return mattered, that they were important events (although I am by no means giving them equal weight), was affirmed not with fussing, not even with words, but with gestures of caring at once practical and symbolic: a real, comfortable ride home in a car that was also a gesture of welcome; a real, professional shave by the local barber that was also a gesture of love. If Tonino had refused that shave to save money or to avoid being the recipient of special treatment, he would surely have wounded his father just as we wounded Tonino, for it is in the unacknowledged, silent taking of such acts that we best give our affection and true understanding of the giver back to him.

The regions of Emilia and Romagna are both known for their spirit of lavish generosity, abundance, human warmth. They are renowned for their cuisine, for their populist (and leftist) politics, for their strong attachment to the earth. Yet, in the mountains of Romagna, in the innumerable little villages hidden away and hard to access, there are also traditions that have little to do with exuberant materiality. There are old beliefs and old stories of witches and seers and magic, of realms unseen and unknowable by the common eye or mind. The earth is filled with poetry, and people are themselves poetic characters in the operatic spectacle of everyday life.

Tonino Guerra's strongly Romagnole qualities of generous activism and magical fantasy came together in the mid-1980s in a series of civic projects dedicated to his native area. He had for many years enjoyed drawing and painting, and this 'hobby' came to the fore in a number of posters designed and written by Guerra, in which he mixes messages of ecological kind, opinions on how best to preserve the traditions of the region, concrete advice for the organization of artistic events designed to enrich the life of all citizens, and especially the young. One of the posters (which were actually posted throughout the area) suggested that a fruit tree be planted on the shores of the local river at the birth of each child so that 'in a few years a great forest of flowers will be created that will stretch from the sea to the Verucchio bridge.'

Guerra's poetical activism did not end here. In and near Santarcangelo, he oversaw a number of projects such as the creation of a Garden of Forgotten Flowers and the preservation of some of the tiny chapels scattered through the hills. In his hometown Guerra had benches put in all around the steep streets so that old people could rest and, perhaps most beautiful of all, he had tile plaques designed by local artists affixed here and there throughout the town on which were recorded the sayings, stories, and little poems of local folk. I remember reading many of them on our stroll with Tonino and Lora in 1989, and immediately feeling the magic of these quirky, funny, unforgettable voices that made a walk through town a walk through poetry itself.

In very recent times — the last five years or so — Guerra has moved closer to his roots and to the land he loves by undertaking the restoration of an ancient house in the tiny mountain town of Pennabilli, some winding kilometers from Santarcangelo. When I saw him the last time, in 1991, he was deeply involved in the restoration project and was spending less and less time in his apartment on the main square of his hometown. The house in Pennabilli is perched high atop a hill overlooking the beautiful valley below, and it is a place of sheer enchantment, filled with flowers and plants, artworks and found objects, the exuberant chaos of creativity and the peaceful order of affection and love. Guerra himself had visibly aged and he was more in his gruff mood than his sweetly lyrical one.

I had again come with a friend, this time someone who did not speak Italian and who spent most of the time rather confused about where Tonino was rushing us off to in our rented car (to the Garden of Forgotten Flowers; to lunch in a small restaurant that serves almost exclusively the local seminarians and priests and in the kitchen of which the town's head 'witch', an ancient woman speaking what was to me a completely unintelligible language, read my palm; to a miniscule church in the almost abandoned village of Secchiano nearby, and so on). It was clear that he wanted us to take in this world of his in the few hours we spent there, wanted us to understand its beauty and its uniqueness and its magical soul, almost as if it and he might disappear at any moment, never again to be seen and felt and lived.

The poems included in this volume have a similar intensity and poignancy. The story of the two old brothers and their world recounted in *Il miele* is, as Italo Calvino wrote:

> a book that becomes more beautiful with every passing year, one that in a hundred years everyone will learn Romagnole dialect in order to read.

The story of the solitary man in his hut told in *La capanna* is at once a timeless tale of the individual's need for connection and a completely contemporary portrait of existential anguish and alienation. The third *poema* or long narrative poem, *Il viaggio*, is a love story in which the old couple Rico and Zaira make their one and only trip to see the sea, remembering their life together as they travel. These plotlines reveal nothing of the power of these visions, however, and it is only in reading them that the world they convey is seen and felt in all of its human complexity, humor, tragedy, and truth.

If very few of us can read Guerra's poetry in the original dialect and some more of us can at least read the Italian versions, many more readers will now be able to enter into this astounding poetry through the lovingly wrought English translations of Adria Bernardi. Herself a writer of great talent, Adria also brings to her versions a personal sense of connection with Emilia-Romagna, the region of her ancestors, and so craft and feeling have come together to give us the words contained in this volume. The publication of this book is an event that fills me with personal and professional joy, personal because of my affection for and admiration of poet and translator both, professional because of my long-standing desire as an Italianist to have one of Italy's most precious cultural treasures better known on these shores. Tonino, you might not have liked your one and only visit to America, but here you are again, thank heavens, and I extend our welcome — and our thanks. And to Adria, *grazie infinite* for having extended the *viaggio* from the shores of the sea to across and beyond it, by means of the art of translation, itself a carrying across that seeks to transcend boundaries and open worlds.

Rebecca West
University of Chicago

Part One

A Trilogy of Return and Departure

I abandon Rome
The peasants
abandon the land
The swallows
abandon my town
The faithful
abandon the churches
The millers
abandon the mills
The people of the mountains
abandon the mountains
Grace
abandons men
Some
abandon everything

I

The Honey

To my mother
and my father
to my grandmother
and my grandfather
to my great-grandparents
and to all those
who spoke
only in dialect

First Canto

When I turned seventy and four days,
    I took a train away
as fast as I could. I couldn't stand it anymore,
    staying in the city
with all those antsy people.

Now I'm here in my hometown, at my brother's.

It's full of empty houses. From the twelve hundred
    who lived here,
we're down to nine: Me, who just arrived,
la Bina, Pinèla the *contadino,* my brother who stayed
in the old house, *la* Filomena with her imbecile son,
and three pensioners who sit on the stairs in the piazza
and worked at one time as shoemakers.

The others went who-knows-where: America, Australia,
    to Brazil,
where crazy Fafin went hunting with a knife
and killed a jaguar thinking it was a cat.
In nineteen hundred and twenty a big group
    of stonemasons,
after six months of travelling with their heads
    hanging over the side of a boat
looking at the sea and the water of a river
    that never ended,
arrived at the Great Wall of China
which was falling apart everywhere,
and they needed men who worked with their hands.
Before he disappeared forever, Bina's father,
    who was one of them,

sent news once a year
that later they called 'The Letters from China.'
    The first one asked
about a goat that had a fever the day he left,
the second said that he had eaten a snake,
the third talked about a woman who sewed on
    his buttons,
the fourth was full of scribbles like a chicken makes
in the mud, to show that he was now Chinese
and that he had forgotten everything, even words.
My parents never moved from the house: my father
    sold charcoal
and my mother kept the accounts on a sheet
    of yellow paper.
Given that she didn't know how to read or write,
    she made thin lines
for skinny people and circles for the fatter clients.
She kept the numbers in her head and when they had paid
she cancelled them out with a cross.

Here the air is good and the water comes from the
    ditches,
no cars at all and the dogs are stretched out
    in the middle of the streets.

Canto Two

This morning I was hardly out the gate
when it seemed like I had left something in the house.
I got two steps toward the apricot-tree
and then I went back inside.

Now that I have nothing to do
I sit near the window
and ask myself: do you want this? Do you want that?

I burned all the pages of the books, the calendars,
the geography maps. For me, America
is no more, Australia nothing,
China is an odor in my head,
Russia, a white spiderweb,
Africa, a glass of water that I dreamed about.

For two or three days I have been following around
    Pinèla the peasant
who's looking for honey from wild bees.

Canto Three

My brother works at the telegraph office in
   the station
where no trains have passed in forty years;
they took away the tracks during the war
when they needed iron for the cannons.

He sits there and waits. But no one ever calls
and he doesn't call anyone. The last telegram
to arrive came from Australia,
addressed to Rino from Fabiòtto who's six feet under.

The day that I went to look for him, my brother
was under the iron shelter
with his hands in his pockets, sitting in the middle
   of an aria
being chirped pizzicato by birds flying off in the distance.

The track where the trains used to pass
is covered with weeds. Now, a chicken is coming down
   toward us
and passes without even turning its head to look back.

Canto Four

So then, one Sunday all the sheep stopped eating:
they stood there with their heads hanging over the field
and it looked like they were asleep. Monday, the same.
On Tuesday, they didn't even want to drink.
    A month passed
and their legs became little sticks holding up
    empty carcasses,
with their eyes rolling back in their heads above
    the snout.
They fell to the ground one at a time, and the wool,
when you touched it, turned to dust.

Every morning, *la* Filomena told her son
the story about the thirty sheep she doesn't have
    anymore.
And he stands there with his mouth open;
    he's forty years old
but he doesn't look it and can't even grow a mustache.
To save him from the women who danced in his head
    naked
and to keep him from masturbating all day long,
she told him he was a knight of the Lord. But the sword,
    where is it?
You have to wait until it falls from the sky. And he waits
    for it
and, in the meantime, his mother repeats the story
    about the sheep.

Nearby, there are white boulders you can sit on
that rolled down into the fields when the mountain
    exploded

below Perticara and everything rained down from the sky.
Afterwards, the white boulders got up and went toward
    home. They say that sometimes
they creep along the grass and line up behind each other
    like they were those dead sheep.

Canto Five

Pirìn, of the Évi family, has his father's name
who in his time had his grandfather's,
at any rate, the Pirìns going back in the Évi family never
 end,
and they all made honey
with the odor of mint.
Their house is halfway up the hill,
far from town and from the valley.

You don't know this but, in America, in the spring,
there are trains that go through plains that are
 covered with apple- and peach-trees,
and they carry hives with bees
that pimp from flower to flower
because the branches can't move to make love
and can't drip into the bells of the flowers.

So this is the trade Pirìn plies in the spring:
he carries the beehives all around the countryside
and then he waits in the shade for the behinds of the bees,
which are greedy and impatient, to impregnate the flowers.
This is why fruit grows,
otherwise there wouldn't be any apples, or peaches, or
 anything.

Canto Six

La Bina lived in a shack
on the crooked street and she would take a goat
on a walk along the ditches.
Nobody was sure whether she was a man or a woman:
she had teats, but she had a mustache too
and mountain boots.
When we were kids, we tried to see
if there was something underneath her skirt,
but she kept her legs closed tight
wrapped up in long underwear.

It's not believed that she ever went with a man
or even an animal, but they say that
she let the oldest of the three American sisters
pull milk from the teat of the goat.
She said in a low voice: 'Squeeze it in your hand, hold it hard,
don't stop.' And sometimes she covered the hands
of the girl with her own and she did the last jerks with her
to show that there is always a drop of milk
    at the bottom of a teat.

Now *la* Bina is almost one hundred years old. She walks
behind the goat and doesn't look anyone in the face.

Canto Seven

Pidio had a wife
who every Saturday washed clothes in the fountain,
and at noon he would give her a hand
and would wring the sheets
in the middle of the street
until they were thick, white snakes
that dripped on the ground.

Now that he doesn't have his wife anymore
a blackbird keeps him company
and he spends his evenings in the piazza
with Gepi and Nano, the other two shoemakers,
and every day he sings, in a whisper,
'Love forbids you' from Giordano's *Fedora*.

Canto Eight

This year the dead leaves have stayed attached
   to the branches
because there is not a breath of wind
and the trees look like little flames in a blaze.

Below Montebello, down along the Marecchia, is a
   convent
that has been closed for a hundred years
with a courtyard in the back that is full of walnut-trees.

My brother and me slipped in through a hole in the wall
so we could walk underneath those trees
that held up a red cloud in their branches.
When we rang the bells, the air moved
and jostled the leaves
and the walnut-trees were all stripped in an instant.

Canto Nine

It must have been raining a hundred days,
   and the water that saturated
the roots of all the plants
Reached the library and soaked all the holy words
which were closed up inside the convent.

When the good weather came,
Sajat-Novà, who was the youngest monk,
got a ladder and took all the books up to the roof,
out in the sun. Then he waited for the warm air
to dry the wet paper.

There was a month of good weather
and the monk kneeled down in the courtyard
waiting for the books to give some sign of life.
And finally one morning the pages started
to rustle slightly in the breeze.
It sounded like a swarm of bees had arrived on the roof
and he started to cry because the books were talking.

Canto Ten

There's nobody living anymore
in the pink house in front of the field
where they used to have the horse fair.
The shutters creak and are falling apart piece by piece
and inside there's a peach-tree growing
from a pit that somebody threw away.

It used to be the house that belonged to the three
    American sisters,
the daughters of that crazy Fafin who went to Brazil,
and who made a trip from Genoa in a carriage,
and he arrived here after three days,
without a coin in his pocket.

The oldest of the three sisters one morning
drowned in the fountain, naked,
with her hair covering her face,
the second, they say they saw in a whorehouse in Ferrara;
the third, who was the one I liked,
one day when there was a dance with a gramophone
danced with my brother, who held her tight
under her arms, and I, head down,
looked at the tiles, all white and yellow.

Canto Eleven

Two days ago, which was the first Sunday
   of November,
there was a fog you could cut with a knife.
The trees were white with frost, and the streets
   and countryside
looked like they were covered with sheets.
   Then the sun came out
and dried the universe, and only the shadows
were still wet.

Pinèla was tying together the vines of the garden rows
with blades of dried grass that he kept behind his ears.
While he worked, I talked about the city,
about my life that had passed in a flash
and that I was afraid of death.

Then he stopped all the noise he was making with his
   hands
and only then could you hear a little sparrow singing
   far off.
He said to me: Why afraid? Death's not so bad,
it only comes once.

Canto Twelve

If it rains it seems like the water is washing your bones,
but if hail hits your shoulders,
it's like a swarm of grasshoppers jumping.
Fog cancels even thoughts
and they stay like lit candles
burning in the brain.

Two or three nights ago the snow covered
the streets and fields
and in the morning me and my brother
saw that there were big footprints
but they weren't from something I recognized. A bear?
They started at the first houses at the edge of town
and ended all of a sudden in the middle of the piazza,
almost like it had flown away.

Canto Thirteen

Ever since I was a boy I liked canes
and I used to steal them from the river
when they were still green.
Then I would spread them out in the sun all summer
and would take them up to the loft, light
as an aria of mosquitoes.

In the winter
when your bones creaked from the cold
and the cats would go up into the apricot-tree to cough,
I would run up into the loft.
and put my hands in the middle of all the warm canes
which still had the sun on them.

Canto Fourteen

The good weather arrived
with a bee that knocked at the windows.
La Bina took off her shoes and she walked
barefoot behind her goat.
The sun threaded the eye of the needle
that Filomena held in her hand.
Pinèla the *contadino* said, Enough!
and he buried his spade in the ground.
Even my brother stopped working
but every so often he would get up from his chair
because he thought he heard a ways away the telegraph
    tapping.
I saw a new blade of grass in the courtyard
which was pushing its head out from under the crust of
    dirt
to make me feel older.
So I crushed it
like it was a cockroach in the house.

Canto Fifteen

Toward the end of March
there was a black cloud above the valley and mountains.
A still cloud
that didn't go forward or backwards.
Sometimes it was round and then it would get long
on top and take the shape of a barrel,
a stack of straw or a snake that never ended;
otherwise, it turned into a delicate fan
that made the whole sky seem filled with flies.
Me, my brother, and there were others too,
thought that they were starlings that came from Russia.
Then it became a dark ball, heavy,
the color of lead, and it made an oval shadow
over the valley. It started to touch the ground
but then it went back up and where it stopped
there were clear specks, almost like ashes after fires.
And so like this, little by little, the whole valley
which was green from the grass, and leaves and grains,
became white like those faces that are afraid,
until the cloud bounced away, over the mountains,
and it wasn't seen again.

What were they, grasshoppers?

Canto Sixteen

At one time a bunch of people used to come
 to do penance
at the Bridge of the Candles, and they asked for grace
for soldiers at war, for love stories,
for illness, to get some money, for youth, for hidden wishes,
for example a lot of them couldn't get it up anymore,
if they said, Ready? it responded, No!
All you had to do was go over the bridge, down as far
as the cross at the mill, with one lit candle,
 without it going out.
But the wind blew, a little breeze that came down
from the mountains, and their hands got tired
from keeping the flame covered, and so
 the people would try, and try again,
for a month, a year . . .
One old woman got as far as the bottom
but her clothes caught fire and so all her efforts went up
 in smoke.
It was because of this awful thing that people
ended the devotion and nobody comes anymore.

Last Sunday, I glanced at the bridge
and I saw Filomena's son, the slow one,
with a lit candle in his hand.
The flame was straight up-and-down and there wasn't
 even a breeze
coming down along the river. What was he asking for grace for?
A normal life or to go on with his head mixed up?
Before getting to the cross at the mill,
which was right there, just two steps away,
he stopped moving and blew out the flame.

Canto Seventeen

My brother walks with his hands behind his back,
if he eats he puts his big elbows on the table,
he ties his shoe putting his foot
on the rung of the chair, if he washes his face
he complains and exhales and grumbles about the cold;
his mustache is just so and he even wears his hat in bed.
When he turns, he turns all in one piece
like he's stiff.
The movements of people from another time are in him:
he lights his match on the sole of his shoe
and he holds the handle of the spoon in a closed fist.

Every so often he stops dead in his tracks to stare
at a corner of the room, squeezing his eyes shut,
and farts come out that sing
like our father's.

Canto Eighteen

When the blackbird escaped from Pidio
   the shoemaker
we waited for it in the courtyard
and every time a shadow passed
it seemed like it was him. But it wasn't.

Then one evening, there was something black
bobbing at the top of the hedge of canes
and it looked at us with little eyes that were like dagger
   points.
So we moved away from the window
and pretended to pull back the chairs.

Canto Nineteen

One morning in the summer I stopped in the sun
and I saw that the streets
were full of people like there used to be
on the day of the silk market.
The cocoons were in sacks
and the aprons of the women billowed.
But it lasted only a moment
and, in fact, I was just a single nail
in the piazza that made a warm shadow.

Canto Twenty

At first the raindrops made the branches nod
and we stayed inside behind the window waiting
for the rain to wash the leaves that were hidden.
Then it rained, rain that God sent,
and so we put a glass on the ledge outside
to measure in centimeters how much water fell.

At four the sun came out
and the glass outside the window glistened
because it was filled all the way up to the rim.

Me and my brother each drank half
and then we compared it to the water from the well:
the water from the sky is more slippery
but it smells like lightning.

Cantèda vintéun

Al fòi de' barcòcal agli éva cmóinz a caschè
a lói e pu d'agòst fina a setèmbar.
A s s'émmi mèss a tóli sò óna a la vólta
e a s divertémmi a cuntèli a vòusa èlta;
éun e' géva mélla, mélla òna, mélla dò e mélla trè
e cl'èlt e cuntinuéva, mélla e quàtar, mélla zóinch e mélla sì.
L'éra una cantiléna ch'la duréva da la matóina a la sàira.
Ch'a n'émm rimpói tri sach.

Mo una matóina e' mi fradèl l'à smèss da lavurè
par dal rasòun ch'u n'à détt a lè par lè
dop a i ò savéu ch'u s l'éra ciapa
parchè scherzànd a i ò dè de pataca
par una fòia ch'u n'éva cuntè.
Mè avéva détt: domélla e dò e léu domélla e quatàr
E la domélla e trè duv'èla?
Basta, a sémm stè dis dè sénza discòrr. A s'alzémmi
vulténdsi al spali, a magnémmi a tèsta basa
e intènt al próimi nèbbi e l'aqua fóina
al féva un vàil sla scóina de capòt.
La sàira a butémmi cal fòi, una manèda prón,
se fugh e a stémmi a quardè la fiamba.

Canto Twenty-One

The leaves of the apricot-tree started to fall
in July, through August and into September.
We started to pick them up one at a time
and amuse ourselves counting them in a loud voice:
One would say: one thousand one, one thousand two, one thousand three
and the other one would continue: one thousand four, one thousand five
one thousand six.
It was a sing-song that lasted from morning to night
and in this way we filled three sacks.

But one morning my brother stopped working
for reasons he didn't say at first.
Later I found out he was mad
because, joking around, I had made a fool of him
over a leaf he hadn't counted.
I had said: Two thousand two, and he said: Two thousand four.
And two thousand three, where did it go?
Enough said. We didn't talk to each other for ten days.
We got up in the morning and turned our backs to each other;
we ate with our heads looking down.
Meanwhile the first fog and drizzle
dropped a veil over the back of my coat.
In the evening we threw those leaves into the fire,
taking turns, a handful at a time,
and we sat there staring at the flame.

Canto Twenty-Two

When, during the autumn,
there were naked trees,
one night, a cloud
of birds arrived
worn out,
and they stopped on the branches.
And it seemed like the leaves had come back
fluttering in the wind.

Canto Twenty-Three

This morning my brother was looking
for something in the drawers; he rummaged everywhere:
first, in the wardrobe, he looked into the pockets
of jackets and coats, and then, throwing his whole body into it,
he pulled everything out of the dresser.
He even turned the kitchen upside down.
He wandered from room to room
without seeing me.
When he started to ransack my bed,
at that point, I said: What do you want?
I don't know. At first I needed a nail,
then a button, then I wanted to make myself some coffee,
and now I want you to say something,
even if it's something silly.

Canto Twenty-Four

The cunt is a spiderweb
a funnel of silk
the heart of all flowers;
the cunt is a door
going who knows where
or a wall
you have to knock down.

There are happy cunts
cunts that are totally crazy
cunts that are wide or tight
worthless cunts
chatterboxes that stutter,
and those that yawn
and don't say a word
even if you kill them.

The cunt is a mountain
white with sugar,
a forest entered by wolves,
it's a carriage that pulls the horses;
the cunt is an empty whale
filled with black air and fireflies;
it's the prick's pocket,
its nightcap,
an oven that burns everything.

The cunt when it's time
is the face of God,
his mouth.

Everything in the world comes out from the cunt
the trees, the clouds, the sea
and men come out one at a time
from every race.
It's from the cunt that even the cunt comes out.
Praise the cunt.

Canto Twenty-Five

For a month we stayed at the window
leaning on our elbows and looking out at that piece of earth
enclosed inside the hedge. And summer came.
Now we go out on the streets of town
without speaking or looking at each other,
as if we weren't walking together.
Sometimes the streetlights around the piazza
stay lit until noon
because every so often, those in the bigger town
who control the lights
forget about us,
and in the sunlight the street lamps
seem like crazed fireflies.
The paths that were covered with loose stones
when they were new
are soft now from the grass under each step.
In the evening we stretch out on the ground
and caress the blades in the cracks,
which are sparse, like the hair of an old woman's head.

Canto Twenty-Six

I had put up a little hut
and I stayed there all day looking at the river
sitting on a chair.

One evening I saw
a white duck,
escaped from my brother's flock,
going down into the water;
his house is right at the spot
where the river
comes down from the mountain.

Later, there was the second duck,
the third, the fourth,
one per week,
and at that point I understood
that these were messages
my brother had sent me.

One morning
the whole flock
all the ducks together,
came down into the water,
next to the hut.
So I closed myself up in the house
out of fear it was bad news.
But I fell out of bed,
and my brother turned on the light.

Canto Twenty-Seven

Hands in my pockets, hands out of my pockets.
Walk to the back of the bedroom.
Look inside the cracks in the wall.
See if there are any cockroaches who are asleep.
Back to bed and sit down
while my brother lies.

Later we went outside
and stood in the middle of the long road
that runs beside the canes.
To one side, where the mountains are, the sun was setting,
and to the other side where the sea is,
    the full moon was growing
on the back of a mule.
They were two things that mirrored each other
and we looked from one to the other
because it seemed like we were between two suns.

Canto Twenty-Eight

I have the impression that stinginess
isn't a defect if it happens when you're old
when boredom has already settled in the head.
I saved myself from it at seventy
when I started to put out the lights at six at night
and my brother stumbled around everywhere.
Now, I just collect used matches
(You can use them with a cotton ball to clean your ears)
at any rate, from morning to night
I have so much to do:
I want my brother to take it easy with the sugar
in his milk, and as for me, with my sweet tooth for honey,
I have one lick from a teaspoon every Sunday
standing in between the two cupboard doors.
No tablecloths; we make do with a piece of paper
that can be used later to light the fire.
At night, if one of us gets up,
one candle is enough, and the other stays in the dark.
In this way, an hour passes, then two, a month,
and the head keeps working.

Canto Twenty-Nine

There was a voice that woke us up.
It was more of a shriek than a normal voice,
saying a name, maybe my name. We opened the windows
and there wasn't anyone there, not in the bedrooms either,
not in the loft, or under the beds, or in the middle of the street.
Weren't we dreaming? But how can you explain
two people dreaming the same thing?
So then, it was a voice in the dark.
A man's voice or a woman's?

Canto Thirty

We were closed up in the dark for ten days
lying on our beds and not taking one look outside.
We talked about everything, about watermelons growing
 oval-shaped,
about peaches filled with juice, about the swallows that
 are gone,
about the earth that becomes ashes
if it's not mixed with manure.
We talked for an entire night
about different kinds of grain,
especially about Mentana, a type you don't find anymore,
that, even when there was wind, wouldn't spread out,
and, by contrast, there was one kind that was painfully
 slow-growing
that would lie down on the ground quicker than a whore.

At any rate, we were discouraged thinking that the world
was getting worse. But one morning,
we opened the dresser drawer and pulled out
two dress suits that we hadn't worn for a long time.
My jacket and pants fit him,
and his stuff seemed made to order for me.
Without knowing where we were going, I opened the door
and right in front of us, in the field that borders
the road, the cherries were in bloom
and welcomed us into that blue air.
Then me and my brother stopped,
propped ourselves against the steps and without saying a word,
we took our hats off our heads.

Canto Thirty-One

I was in the courtyard and I saw my brother
standing at the window. If I scratched my head,
he scratched his; if I took off my hat,
he took off his; he made all the motions I made:
took off the jacket, the tie, and the shirt,
and stood there with a naked chest as if it were a challenge:
we stood facing each other for ten minutes
and then I turned my back on him and went to the piazza
and he disappeared from the window.

Canto Thirty-Two

Twenty days ago I put a rose in a glass
on top of the little table near the window.
When I noticed that all the leaves
were withered and ready to fall
I sat myself down in front of the glass
to see the moment that the rose died.

I was there one day and one night waiting.

The first petal broke off at nine in the morning
and I let it fall in my hands.
I had never been at a deathbed,
not even when my mother died
and I stood, far away, at the end of the street.

Canto Thirty-Three

This summer those worthless young people arrived,
the ones who stick their noses everywhere
and who are always riding in the backs of trucks
or spread out on barges in search of Africa.
They moved into the house that belonged
to the three American sisters
where the peach-tree between the walls
takes up all the air. They sleep
on the floor wrapped up in rags
and they reach out their hands to pick the fruit.

During the day, they walk barefoot in the empty narrow streets,
they yell and laugh; they throw dust in their faces
and shoot up in their arms.
I'm tired of saying how they ruin everything,
even the grasshoppers who go far, far away
die during their voyage.
Filomena's son, the slow one, went away with them.

Canto Thirty-Four

First, the alarm clock broke,
and then, the big pocket watch that an engineer
gave my brother broke. So then we told time
using the sun rays that filtered into the kitchen
and made streaks on the edge of the cupboard
if it was nine in the morning;
when it got to the glasses, it was exactly noon.
Later, there was a clear mark
that hit against the nails
and moved around the two beds
until it disappeared at six in the evening
into the spiderweb on the ceiling. If it rained
our ears told time
from the noises on the street.
All you needed to know that it was seven in the morning
was to hear *la* Bina passing by behind her goat,
and that when they came back, it was noon.
The three shoemakers eat when the sun begins to go down
and they drag their chairs out of the piazza
while the cicadas stop singing because the dark
scares them. *La* Filomena does her sifting at two in the morning.
One Sunday we were wrong and mixed up six in the evening
and six in the morning, and we knew then
that our ears and all the little wheels inside our heads
were broken.

Canto Thirty-Five

Water, fire, and then ash
and bones in the ashes,
the air trembles around the Earth.
Where are the green leaves, the grass, the peas
that the fingers of women pry out of pods?
Where are the roses and the guitar, the dogs and the cats,
the stones and the border hedges,
the mouths that sing, calendars, rivers,
and teats full of milk? Where are the tales
if extinguished candles don't give off light anymore?
Where is Time with the days of the week,
the hours and seconds which beat?
The Sun moves and the shadows of still things shift.
And where am I? Where is Mr. So-and-So?
Venice, which drowned,
is a bunch of bones under the sea.
But there will be a day when a voice comes
 through a door in the sky
and falls down into the dust.
It will command that the man
who invented things of every kind come out:
the wheel, clocks, numbers
and flags on the street.
And then Adam will get up with his head high
and go under that Great Light
to say that the honey that he gave us
was at the end of a sword.

Last Canto

Now the two brothers are buried under the oak tree
near the twisted cross of the contessa
who had forty farms
and a little sidecar with rubber tires.
From Easter until Christmas, they closed themselves in
    completely
and they didn't put so much as a finger up to the window.
Later it became known that one of the two
kept the other in a closet, on bread and water,
stuttering curses at him.
When the nun who was a nurse
pushed the door open
they looked like sacks of garbage.
They didn't even last a week at the hospital.
They were lying on two cots
which were separated by a chair,
not looking at each other,
but they held each other's hand.

II

The Hut

To the people of Naples
who do everything in dialect:
ugly things and beautiful things

1

Ten years ago I saw one of those huts
down below San Giovanni in Galilea
in the middle of fields of sand
where the Rubicon once flowed;
maybe at one time there was a sea
surrounding it
that beat against the cliff where the church sat
and kept it protected.
The hut I saw was called Zangàla's hut;
he was Bigióla's father who in 1884
left with other laborers from Ravenna to drain
those swamps south of Rome
where mosquitoes chased people
in the thickets of reeds, and even the canes trembled with
    fever.
Four hundred eighty people from Romagna went,
including Zangàla
and Giulio Carabini, who was the brother of that
    Penelope
who married Edoardo, the charcoal maker in Santarcangelo.
Twenty percent of them died; even our own Giulio
lost his hide to the mosquitoes.
Zangàla, instead, made it, and when he came back
he began to look for water everywhere
in order to forget the filth he had drunk,
rotten boiled water to be spit out into the ditches.
He would swish the water in his mouth to determine
whether it tasted like iron
or that stink of sulfur that makes you gag,
or if it had the scent of roses and slid blessedly
    between his teeth.

And he built the hut
with other people as a way of being all together
while they wore themselves out working in the fields,
just like Nullo Baldini had recommended
to those who worked to reclaim the marsh.

It was as big as four haystacks of straw put together
and inside was the stall, the pigsty
the alcove for the firewood
the kitchen, the larder,
passages, closets, lumber rooms, the pigeon coop,
bedrooms, hallways that went
to the big room in back
where they would sit up with the dead,
and lofts with floors
covered knee-deep with apples, pears,
medlars and a little of everything else;
there were storehouses of grain
and barrels in the wine cellar.
So many rooms
that from beginning to end
it took a day to look at them,
and the old people
spent the winter
without having to step foot outside,
either the front door or back.

It was a mountain of planks
that covered forty rooms,
closed in above with tin,
rusted gates, metal plates and vats that emptied
water down into the gutters
and deflected lightning bolts
into tubs or onto the sand
that flowed back down into the reeds.

2

Aqua l'era avnéu a pasè l'invéran
un òm si zinquènt'an
ch'un vléva avdài niséun.
Dòp u s'è savéu ch'u s ciaméva Omero,
mo chi ch'l'éra dabón u n'e' savéva
gnénca i cuntadóin
chi era i padréun dla tèra.
Po dès che fóss e' fiul
ad chi sgnuréun che una vólta
i éva tótta la tnéuda
o magari l'era un avuchèd
ch'l'éva da studié un procès
o e' fiul de' calzulèr
quél che studiéva al stèli,
e u s'aspitéva la fóin de mònd
da un mumént a cl'èlt
mo l'éva za sbaiè dò vólti
te spusès: la próima la cantéva
tótt e' dè, la sgònda
la è scapa véa s'un èlt.
Dróinta la capana
u i era quatar lampadóini
e gnénca una radio o la televisiòun.
Omero l'avéva scarghè dla ròba
da un camiòn e pu l'era sparói
da la faza dla zénta.

2

A man in his fifties
who didn't want to see anyone
came here to spend the winter.
They knew he was called Omero
but they didn't know who he really was,
not even the peasants who owned the land.
He could have been the son
of those rich people who owned the land
at one time,
or maybe a lawyer
who had to prepare for a trial,
or the son of that shoemaker
who counted the stars
and from one moment to the next
expected the end of the world, the same shoemaker
who had already made the mistake of marrying twice:
the first sang all day long and never did any work,
the second ran off with another man.
Inside the hut
there were four electric light bulbs
and no radio or television.
Omero unloaded his stuff
from a truck, then disappeared
totally from people's sight.

3

Inside the hut, there were windows, tiny windows, cracks,
blinds, holes and doors (there were more than fifty of them),
and for more than a week Omero
began to look at what was outside to see:
First, the trees that the peasants
had planted around the house — the mulberry they had
planted near the well so that when the women
pulled out the water they wouldn't get sunstroke,
the walnut-tree that kept flies away,
the rattan for making baskets
and hampers, which the old people made during vigils,
the tamarisk to make brooms
that were used to sweep the stalls and the threshing floor,
the elder-tree to use against tapeworms,
and the reed-thicket that supplied new canes
for the vineyard. All this was still there
but the only thing left of the haystacks
were posts driven into the ground
with loose crossbars
that could no longer hold fodder
in windstorms.
On foggy days, you could see only
the tips of the posts and the rest was under a cloud
raining on the ground, four
black points that looked like drowned
boats, and farther away, you could see, floating
above the clouds,
the bell tower of San Giovanni in Galilea
with the walls of its cemetery
that kept all the iron crosses closed in, up there in the air.

And you could see the edge
of the castle where they say
Francesca of Rimini arrived, visiting relatives,
on a horse with a silver harness
and behind her was her husband's brother,
who was beating all the yellow spring flowers with a cane.
Sometimes the fog erased everything
and the windows were shut against
kilometers and kilometers of damp dust
that kept you from being able to see the shadows that
the reeds made and the red colored leaves of the
    peach-trees
that were falling to the ground.
But you could hear shots up above,
a truck that was going like hell,
and two warplanes
that were flying in the sunlight above the clouds
chasing after each other like madmen.
When they dove headfirst
it seemed like the sky was falling on the hut
and Omero covered his ears with his hands
because the windows and the ground were shaking:
If there is a war, one bomb is enough
to destroy everything between the sea and the mountains
and men will be shadows on the walls.
Early one morning, however,
the countryside was white with frost
as if it had rained milk.
Then the sun came out
and the colors of the earth returned,
although that warm light didn't dry everything,
and Omero, who watched spellbound, looked at a
world turned upside down,
where there were houses and trees with white shadows
dotting the entire plain.

There were also windy days
with tattered cloth and paper being batted around
and pieces of tin cracking,
and stones inside cans rattling
in order to scare away the marmots.
Suddenly the wind
fell to the earth
and was lying among the grass
and fragments of cabbage leaves.
Omero couldn't sleep because of the silence;
he felt like he was falling down into a well
that had no water and no bottom: then he started to yell
to get rid of the cotton ball that was blocking his ears
and it left him alone in the hollowed-out bed.
All at once, the air started to move
beating against the little windows.
The glass of the windows shook,
the cracks whistled and the holes in the wood,
and the whole hut,
began to creak as if it were
a ship going around the world.

4

Inside the four walls
of the farmyard, there were nails
on which to hang all the braided strands of onions and garlic,
and the tobacco leaves, ears of corn, and the cages
of the peasants who went hunting, especially Bigióla
who kept blackbirds, sparrows
and magpies: and he liked the little white snails
gathered near the sea
when there used to be thorny bushes
and those hedges of reeds that separated
the sand dunes
and marked out gardens that looked like handkerchiefs
where, now, there were just four potato plants and one
    watermelon growing.
There aren't any snails there anymore
and everything is ruined
by cement walls
that changed the face
of a a wilderness
in air heavy with salt
where now maggots crossed straw covered with dung
left by horses,
where the sea
comes and goes on the sand
and used to tickle people
who would run to huddle
in the shade under sheets. To get back to the nails . . .
At that time Bigióla and his sons, and down to his grandson
with the eyes like an owl's,
were a band that went hunting and they kept
the cages with the birds in the farmyard

to get air, and at night
they hung up the cages in the passageways.
Who knows where the cages are now.
The nails remained and
you could see them hanging only at certain times
when the sun rose above
and the walls were filled in by shadows
suspended over the walls.
Omero waited for that moment
to watch the black lines
growing longer from the nails,
down, down, down, down to the ground,
and it was always exactly noon.
Then, right away, the sun hid
and the shadows went back into the nails
which disappeared in the light.

5

He fixed meals just for himself
making do with a little: two potatoes
cooked in the ashes, tomatoes,
lettuce and onions cut in half
with a drop of oil, a little salt,
pepper, and then three hours
in the oven of the stove
that had been left behind there in the hut
because the new houses have gas stoves.
He hung bunches of grapes
here and there,
also some medlars
and some sorb-apples that were still green
that he felt each day
to see if they were ripe.
He had brought a box of chestnuts
and he boiled them down a few at a time
and emptied the pot of porridge teaspoon by teaspoon.
Some evenings, if it was colder than usual
he roasted the chestnuts
in the stove, and the air
was filled with the odor of burnt peels
and then he made a big deal of
taking away all the ashes.

6

And one day Isolina came to see him;
she was a peasant's daughter
who wanted to do housework, secretly,
because she had gotten married in the city
to a millionaire who made his fortune in socks
and she couldn't show herself.
She liked to repeat the humiliation
her mother suffered
when she worked as a maid for rich people,
and as a little girl, Isolina
would go with her mother to keep her company.
Then, after the war and all the confusion,
the peasants became owners of the land and built
houses with baths and televisions,
their sons who studied in Bologna
became lawyers and she, who was a young
girl with teats that laughed
in the air, got married in the city,
and she sat all day long in an easy-chair.
Now, at age twenty-five,
she had come to spend the winter
with her family while her husband
was travelling around the world
getting contracts.
When Isolina found out
that there was a man who had come to live
inside the abandoned hut,
a man, maybe, around fifty
who was the son of the people who had owned the land
before the war,
when she found this out,

she went one morning, secretly,
showing up to give him a hand, saying
that she was tired of doing nothing
and that she liked the air of the hut
which she had breathed
when she was a child. And she took off
her shoes and started wiping the floor with a wet rag.
She was bent over and swinging her behind
like those wasps that suck up honey.
And when she squeezed the rag
and let the dirty water drip
into the bucket, at first she wrung
it with all her force
and then she ended up caressing it.
Let's put all the cards out on the table:
it wasn't that she was crazy,
she was happy enough with her husband,
in the final analysis, he was a good lover; however,
since she didn't have to lift a finger
every so often she would think
of the hut and dream
of doing the work her mother did:
cleaning shoes, washing shirts, ironing,
wiping rags over the tiles in the rooms,
dusting the furniture,
wearing out her arms, sweating . . .
'Please, let me do it,'
she asked the first time. 'But don't tell
anyone or it would be a disaster.'
'Now that you are a rich lady
you want to go crazy over dust?'
'I want to! I want to!'
Omero looked at her from a distance
and she said to him while she worked:
'Talk, talk, unburden yourself to me.

Tell me everything about your wife.'
'She was a whore,' Omero answered.
'But it was more my fault than hers,
because I like sluts.'
And she remembered
her grandfather's sister, *la* Nazzarena
who, into her nineties, wrote from Brazil,
where her sons, who became rich,
had sent a kilo of coffee
during the war, and so she wrote
in dialect and each time she repeated
that the biggest disappointment in her life
was to have missed the fair in Verucchio
in nineteen hundred twelve, a whole day
full of people to meet
and having those good laughs that young people have.
But there was the great stream, the Marecchia, and
la Nazzarena was stopped there
with her family on the cart with the cabbages
that they were going to sell to the livestock merchants
and to the musicians in the band — you could see
them on the other side of the river — but you couldn't
    cross over
because there wasn't a bridge anymore:
it had disappeared under water during a storm
that swept trees and drowned pigs
down from the mountain.

7

One night Omero put the bed warmer in bed
and laid down next to it
after having seen that outside it was raining,
a deluge of water
over the countryside;
it seemed like there was
a cloud of dust rising up,
a spiderweb of drops around the hut.
There was warm air from his head to his toes
coming from the fire in the hand warmer,
and he read the story
of a young nun who had lived a thousand years ago:
they had closed her up in a convent
in the mountains against her will,
and so she carried with her for company
a sack full of flowers that she could see
from her house. In that way,
alone in the mountains, inside her cell,
every once in awhile she would put her head
on the sack, which she had made into a pillow,
and she remembered her life as a girl.
When she died, the flowers
were reduced to dust. Even today,
after one thousand years, the pieces that remain
of the sack, give off a strong perfume of roses,
and Omero, in his bed, smells that
odor which seems to jump from the pages of the book
and, in the meantime,
outside the water hits
against the wood of the hut.

8

At any rate, it happened that every so often
Omero and Isolina would see each other
and she would run from one room to the other
dusting and washing the floor. He watched her
and one day said to her: 'Do you hear
how my heart is beating?'
and she, with her hands wet,
nudged his chest with her elbow
and then blushed.
She wouldn't hear of being paid;
more than anything she liked to talk about Bigióla,
who had been given a gold wedding band
by his wife on the day of their wedding,
but the first night
he couldn't sleep because he had the sensation
of never being able to take it off again.
It seemed like it had him by the neck
and was strangling him.
So they tried and tried to take it off
and the finger swelled up like a sausage,
but it wouldn't come off, not with oil,
not even with soap; luckily
at four in the morning
they found a blacksmith in San Giovanni
who cut off the ring.
One Saturday, Omero heard Isolina
peeing in the outhouse
that was among the nettles outside the hut,
a long sing-song that sounded like
a mosquito flying,
and, in fact, not one, but a thousand, mosquitoes

arrived on him
and bit him everywhere
and he swelled up until
something burst in his pants.

9

It started to snow the sixth of December
and it didn't quit, in short, until Christmas.
Omero stayed next to the window
watching those white butterflies
that were falling over the countryside
and inside the barnyard, where the firewood was stacked,
which was enclosed by walls
and as big as a bedroom.
A meter of snow fell
and it looked like a sheet spread out
over the fields and inside the barnyard too.
One day, he amused himself
by dropping heavy things
that made holes in the carpet of snow;
he threw down a ball made of iron,
two stones that weighed God-knows-how-much
and a hammer. Then, down in the courtyard,
there were four black spots that he stared at
as if they were flowers
on a white tablecloth. Then the sun
little by little melted all the snow
down to the bricks, and the holes
he had made disappeared.

10

The first dirty word that he said to her
was said one evening when, without meanness,
they began that business;
then they always used it when talking to each other
as if it were a pinch of salt
in the soup. When she was a girl
she had seen a donkey
who had a penis a meter-and-a-half long,
and he rubbed himself on the ground if he was resting
but if he got up it looked like the shaft of a handcart.
One morning, she was frightened and put her hat
on it. But that day at the sea
she was in the sun without a hat on her head.
One time Omero asked her
if it was true that the old peasant women
peed standing up because they didn't wear
any underwear beneath their skirts; so then she laughed
and started to swing her back
to show that on the skin in back
there wasn't a little line from underwear.
When he asked her to show him her breasts
she didn't want to, didn't want to,
but one afternoon, she was bent over the floor
picking up a hat pin
and he saw two round bocce balls
that looked like two big drops
that ended in a black point;
so he asked her why they were like that. She said
it was the way she was made, even her aunt Zaira
had the same kind, and her grandmother Filomena,
who was a widow for twenty years

and never betrayed her husband.
In fact, that time that Bigióla
came home for Christmas with a fruit
that looked like a gold ball,
a fruit which had never been seen in San Giovanni
    in Galilea,
a Japanese persimmon,
Filomena was dying to taste it,
but when, at eight in the evening,
they cut it up in many little slices
so that everyone could have a little,
she hid in the stall behind the cows
and cried
and refused to put into her mouth a piece of fruit
that her husband had never eaten.
Then she put herself into bed and had
no desire to ever get up again: There was nothing
wrong with her,
but she was tired and she stayed put.
The night before she died, she said
to all her people who were there around her:
'Remember that after us
there won't be any *us* anymore.'

11

He had heard it said that somewhere
there was a long ladder
that was used for a big undertaking
by Bigióla's people, four brothers
who were communists who planted corn
in holes that they made with their fingers;
only the oldest one got married,
the one, who in order to get out of the war,
pretended to go crazy and broke a half-window
over the head of a poor police officer
who was right there among the rows
where the landowner, Signor Domenico,
had gone to sleep at night
to find out if the peasants were stealing.
He was a worthless cunt, Signor Domenico:
one morning at the window of his villa
down at the end of the avenue
he put up a curtain made of pink paper
made of one thousand *lire* notes and the peasants looked
with their mouths dropped open.
The ladder was the same one the kids
used in November to gather
the jujubes from on top of the tree
near the wall which had grown very tall,
and so Bigióla's grandfather
cut the branches of the acacia
to make a ladder that was as long as hunger.
That very same implement
was used by the four brothers
the last night in April of thirty-four
to announce, with a signal,

May Day. That night the four brothers
crossed the fields with the long ladder
bumping against everything they passed
until they arrived below San Giovanni.
The leaned the ladder up against the cliff
and climbed up, up as far as the wall
of the cemetery. Here and there
in the mounds of mud, they planted
little flags made from red paper
which, on the morning of May Day,
fluttered all over San Giovanni.

Omero wandered around
from one room to another
looking to see if the ladder was still there;
instead he found, tacked up on a nail,
Bigióla's bicycle which was reduced to heap
of rusted metal. Bigióla, until he was seventy,
pedalled around like he was a young fellow, then
he got afraid of falling into the ditches.
At eighty, he would go shopping
in San Giovanni, walking his bicycle,
not getting up onto it, holding it close
as if he were giving his arm to someone.
At any rate, the bicycle kept him company,
given that his wife was dead and his children
had so much to do in their own houses. He walked
putting one hand on the handlebar
and he went along so that you could see
he was still in good shape.

12

One time Omero waited inside for Isolina
to tell her he had a crush on her
that he couldn't stand anymore, but she didn't even
look at him, then one Sunday she turned around suddenly
and said to him: 'Maybe you should die of wanting!
But I'm not going to lift up my skirt, and don't hope
that I'm going to come and unbutton your pants
like Zaira did for your father
and pulled out the shirttail and something else
and then their legs bent up in the reed thicket
    among the canes.
All this filth that I saw made me muddled in the head
because I didn't understand if they were fighting or not.
Later, with my husband, I understood, when
I too saw lights glinting in front of my face
turning everything upside down in my head
turning it all into a whirlpool where everything drowned.'
Then she bent over
to wring out the clothes in the washtub,
and Omero, trying to find some peace,
passed the time too stunned to look at anything,
even a cloud in the sky:
where will it all end?
Either faraway near the huts made with plastic,
puffed out like a whale's gut,
where in November they grow tomatoes
and chrysanthemums for the dead
but now they were just rattling around empty
and full of clear air.
Either he held a stone in his hand, or he
came to the big room where babies

used to sleep in rows, and he started
to look at the grass
which had grown in the cracks between the boards
and since there wasn't a sliver of light
that had come in for more than ten years, the grass
had become white
as the hair of an old person, soft to touch
and swaying in a gust of wind.
One afternoon he amused himself
by cutting the grass, until he discovered
a fox sleeping in the corner
who didn't even notice him.
So he closed the door
and tiptoed out so as not to wake it.

One night he dreamed that all the trees in Romagna
were one thousand years old
and covered the avenues, every piazza, the gardens,
and that people were like snails along the pathways
underneath the branches of trees that formed spiderwebs
or that were filled with dry leaves
that rained on the byways.
In the cemetery, as well, there was the shade
made by a sapling planted near the gate
of the tomb where his photograph
had totally faded.
Every so often on clear days
you could look as far as the sea;
the avenue lined by horse-chestnuts, which at one time
took the owners to their villa,
seemed only a few steps away;
but the house wasn't there anymore:
it disappeared during the war.
They only thing left was the avenue
that started at the street

and ended at the gate
that opened to nothing.
Every so often Omero heard chestnuts falling
to the ground and it seemed to him that, there underneath,
his grandfather Domenico was passing by in his gig
to look over the countryside. He used to crack his whip
and scare the peasants who were gathering
mulberry leaves to feed the silkworms.
Even things he had completely forgotten
came to mind:
his sister who ran away from Bologna
with the English official; the sister who was first courted
by the youngest of four brothers who came every night
and played music at the gate of the villa
and they shouted out the window, 'Who is it?'
and he responded, 'Open up, it's me.'
as if it was the most normal thing in the world to make love;
but she didn't want him
and their parents never opened up the gate.
After he had kept waiting a good while —
even in the rain, even during the war when the owners
left the villa and went to live in Bologna —
his mother came to get him and said:
'That's enough now, let's go home,
who is she, anyway?'
And arm-in-arm, she took him away.
But one fine day the Americans
destroyed the villa because they thought
it was full of German generals; but instead
there was one young soldier
about sixteen years old
with hair the color of corn
who died under the bricks. Given that the women
knew he was named Fritz,
someone had named a hunting dog after him.

When the war was over Bigióla went all around
the countryside collecting those hats made of iron
that the Germans threw out as they were running away
and he used them, turned upside down,
for chicken feed.

13

One day Isolina arrived
with her eyes coming out of her head:
the radio and television
had talked about the earthquake in Persia,
with the dead, the dust, palaces in ruins,
heaps of garbage, soldiers who gave
pomegranates and melons
to thirsty people, the children who were jumping
on top of bedsprings and pigs scrounging
around everywhere; Isolina was afraid for her husband
who had gone to Africa
to exchange the stock of socks for some petroleum.
But what do they have to do with each other —
 Africa and Persia?
She didn't want to hear any of it, and she said that
 earthquakes
travel through the ground, that there was a fissure
 that went all
around the earth, and that sometimes they start in one
 cavity
and travel across the world.
'It could even come here,' she said. 'There was one two
 hundred
years ago in April, and even earlier before that, and there
 was one
during the war of eighteen, a jolt that knocked all the bell
 towers
down to the ground.' When the electric lights started
swinging from the ceiling she threw herself in his arms
and said that it was the end of the world
and that the house was trembling because of the desire

they had, and she stripped herself naked in an instant.
Then Omero went to close the door
but his legs shook on the stairs.
He bolted the door shut
and already he imagined being inside of her, but instead
his mind was against it and told him: 'If you have
    courage,
don't go back, give it all up,
what's the use? Open the door and get out of here.'
He opened the door without believing it,
then he took two steps, then two more,
and he walked until six in the evening
and in a loud voice he said:
'I'm a madman' — but he walked and walked
and the street brought him to the station.
He left by train, but he had such a desire
to make love that he could hardly bear it.

III

The Journey

To the Marecchia
which is born
on Mount Zucca
and arrives at the Adriatic
in the hopes
that many eyes
notice it

1

Un dè d'utòubar i s'è mèss a caminé
te fióm éulta i santìr ad sabia e dri
cal linguètti d'aqua ch'al sèlta tra i sas.
De mèr u i avéva zcòurs piò di tótt
una piscèra che fina e' melanovzentquarènta
la i arivéva a là sò in biciclètta,
pu la s'è fata e' sidecàr e la purtéva
al casètti pini 'd giàz e pès
e la racuntéva ch'u i era dal bés-ci
dróinta l'aqua piò grandi dal munghèni
e che dal vólti u s'arenéva dal baléni
ch'l'era dal muntagni ad chèrna
sòura la sabia.
Rico e la Zaira i n éva mai vést e' mèr
che in linea 'd aria, pasénd da i sentìr de fióm,
l'era a trénta chilometri gnénca.
Adès ormai ch'i avéva quèsi utènt'an
i s'è decióis a fè che viàz ad nòzi a pì,
ch'i éva armànd d'an in an. I stéva
a Petrèlla Guidi, un ghèt ad chèsi vèci
in dò che ogni tènt u i era di cavàl
ch'i scapéva dal mèni de manischèlch
e i féva al lózzli sòtta i zòcal mat
e 'd nòta u i era l'udòur de pèn ch'i l cuséva
te fòuran e t al sentévi da dróinta te lèt,
ranicéd ti béus di mataràz ad fòi. Rico
l'à fat e' barbìr quèsi stènt'an ma i óman
mal dòni e pu e' tuséva i sumàr e al pigri;
la Zaira la féva al fazèndi 'd chèsa
e dal vólti la tnéva e' cadóin dl'aqua
in dò che l'artésta e' lavéva e' pnèl.

1

One day in October, they started to walk
in the river along the banks of sand and next to
those little tongues of water that skip among the stones.
She had spoken to them most of all of the sea —
the fishseller, who until nineteen forty
would arrive up there on a bicycle
(afterwards she used a sidecar) and brought up
crates full of ice and fish
and told them there were beasts
in the water bigger than milk-cows
and sometimes they ran aground, these whales
that were mountains of flesh
covering the sand.
Rico and *la* Zaira had never seen the sea
which as the crow flies, following the river roads,
was thirty kilometers, not even.
And now, at eighty,
they decided to take on foot the honeymoon trip
that they had put off year after year. They lived
in Petrella Guidi, a hamlet of old houses
where every so often horses
escaped from the blacksmith's hands
and sparks would fly from their frenzied hooves.
At night, in their bed, sunk into their mattress of leaves,
they smelled the odor of bread
they had baked in the oven. Rico
had been a barber for seventy years, for women
and men, and afterwards he sheared donkeys and sheep;
la Zaira cleaned houses
and sometimes she held the basin of water
in which the artist washed his brush.

2

It was an autumn with days
that seemed like summer and there were bunches of grapes
sweeter than sugar. The lane of cherry trees,
which from Petrella when they flowered
seemed to throw snow into the sky,
now let leaves fall onto the ground
and underfoot there was a piece of something sticking out,
and Rico, toddling along, heard something creak:
it was a wooden thing that seemed like a big frog.
But who was it who threw away this violin?
La Zaira recalled a man that played, a gypsy,
who arrived for the fair of Sant'Antonio,
and just maybe under those leaves, he is buried too,
given he could be ninety or more.
They sat for two hours and *la* Zaira twisted around
and slid off her wedding band
which had become large on her, and she said
that maybe he died sitting down
and that he didn't even know it;
but Rico thought of it another way:
'They like to say it's beautiful to die in your sleep —
you need to die roaring against it all.'
Afterwards, they started to eat something they had carried
in a basket and drank from the bottle of water
they had filled in the *lavadeur*, the fountain
where at one time all the women of Petrella Guidi
pounded clothing against stone edges
and the whole time they sang and rinsed sheets,
which together with their husbands they wrung
before hanging them over
the hedges nearby.

3

They went inside an abandoned mill
with flour dust on top of ladles,
sieves, measuring bowls, sacks, cords,
and the wooden troughs which from the hole above
threw off sword-blades of water against
the wheel that turned the millstone.
But below, now, there were
shovels not nailed up, just lying there like spoons
outside soup. Rico, who all his life
had cut the miller's hair,
and *la* Zaira, who had held the basin of water for him,
stretched out on a bunch of sacks,
being that they were tired, very tired . . .
'Sometimes what enters my head
is that summer afternoon
that we fanned ourselves with pieces of paper
outside the door and there was someone
throwing buckets of water onto the street.
Then all those white butterflies
that came from upriver arrived
and they settled everywhere
and things around there
took on the color of milk: doors,
windows, walls, and those of us who were sitting around
looked like big lumps of rag dolls covered with chalk.
No one breathed so as not to disturb
the butterflies which maybe were tired
of the journey and were resting
to go God-knows-where. Then an odor
of hay came down from the mountains
and all the butterflies rose up together into the air

and cast a shadow over us
as we watched them with our mouths open.'
'Me, instead, sometimes what comes to my mind,'
    said *la* Zaira,
'is that when I was a girl,
I stood at the window and laughed
if you stumbled on stones while looking at the sky.'

4

In the river there were sand pits
where they saw, here and there,
stones, so Rico piled them up in the middle
with a stick because it made him sad
to see them alone.
Then they stopped to watch the machine crushing rock
with all its shovels that dumped
the gravel on a conveyor belt that carried the material
to be crushed in the hammer-wheel,
and there were bins that sifted and divided piles
of stones until on one side
there was the rough gravel and on another the finest sand.
Rico and *la* Zaira sat under that cobweb
of iron that dripped water, and there were trucks
being filled with stuff under iron funnels.
The man who opened and closed the reservoir
was a stonebreaker from Petrella Guidi,
one of those who used to crush gravel with a hammer
and lived all summer under the shadow of a canopy
made of sackcloth. When the rock-crushing machines
    appeared,
the stonebreakers left Petrella; but now, with all the gravel
being eaten by machines
the water of the river is slipping away to the sea,
without stopping one moment to feed the wells
which all around there are drying up
like holy water fonts
in the abandoned churches.
This man who was from Petrella Guidi
didn't remember anything anymore about his town:
now he was fine where he was

and he didn't even ask what had become of
his people: for him Petrella Guidi
was an odor of rosemary
so strong that it hit you from behind.

5

They came to a woods in front of a church
whose roof, in seventy, had fallen
under the weight of the snow, and for ten years
there had been only external walls and piles of broken
    roof tiles,
debris, fragments of bricks, and on the inside young toughs
had drawn dirty pictures with charcoal:
cunts and dicks that flew in the air,
as if they went from the Madonna painted
above the altar who no longer had a face
because, maybe, in order not to see all that filth
she had made herself fade away
and she remained a white spot of lime.
Fortunately, with time, the walls fell
and only the facade was standing, smooth and naked
of ornamentation, and in front and behind, wild grass
had grown knee-high. During recent days,
the priest, using a long ladder, had made holes
every meter, starting at the top and working to the ground.
They were niches in the facade as big as fists
and now he was painting them with lime
which was dripping onto his apron.
Rico and *la* Zaira, without even discussing it,
began to give him a hand, then they helped him put
crumbs of bread in the holes,
and little glasses of water, some leaves of lettuce,
some corn and grain,
then all three hid themselves in the cemetery
where nobody was buried anymore,
and now, on the surrounding walls, there were some red
    and sky blue

cornices of plaster, empty and without any photos.
From behind there they looked to see if the birds
went to eat and sleep in the holes
because the priest wanted them to sing
from the top of the facade so that on Sunday the *contadini*
would be more inclined to be silent in the face of this
    miracle.
The first to settle up there was a blackbird,
then the sparrows arrived and rested with their heads
sticking outside the holes,
then the pigeons, an owl, half asleep,
and robins which shit all over the wall.
As night was falling, they started to sing
and the facade took on a more holy air.
The priest — whose hair was matted because
he had lain all day on a pillow
fighting off the hollowness that put him to sleep
    from morning to night —
now was happy, and pulled out some slices
of cheese, some *piada* and a little wine.
And they talked about a little of everything,
even the sea which the priest
had seen many times when he brought
the children of the *contadini* by bus to the seashore,
and even now he could not understand why
the water pretends to advance:
'They like to say it's the fault of the moon!'
They were ready to go to sleep and *la* Zaira asked
to confess herself and so they went outside
to the front door which was still in the facade, and he
heard her confession. One from here, one from there,
the words passed through the cracks. She told him
that forty years ago she had betrayed her husband,
    one time,

with a man who played the violin at the fair of Sant'Antonio,
a wanderer who wore a *borsalino* hat
with a greasy brim and who played at high mass;
it could be he was a gypsy because he had that
    glowing skin
the color of coffee, like stones held for a long time in your
    hand.
Rico meanwhile slept with a cigar in his mouth,
as always, and she pulled it out little by little,
otherwise the ashes would fall on him,
    and maybe even the ember.

6

For penance the next morning
la Zaira got down on her knees in front of the facade
and listened to the birds for an hour,
just as the priest had assigned,
and right after he preached to her and said
that life is longer for those who are willing to laugh
and then he started talking about Mary Magdalen
who was a nothing
but who became what-she-became
and performed miracles like crazy.
Rico searched among the nettles
and wild bushes above where the church had stood at one
   time;
he looked for those bunches of lemon-scented verbena
you put behind the ear
until they are dried, and that in Petrella
give off that scent of lemon and mint while he worked.
The priest sat on top of the bricks
and nearby *la* Zaira sat, too.
Finally, Rico came up to them
to give him the leaves of those plants
he had found where there once was
an altar, and all together
they closed their eyes to better smell the perfume.

7

At Pietracuta, a hamlet right along the river,
there is a party and a group of Polish artists
performing theater with some red paper
that is stuck onto the walls, doors, windows,
the street, in effect, the whole town has put on a new face.
And then they hand out some white flags
to those who are looking on, and the *contadini*
wave them in the middle of all this red stuff.
With the parading finished, the artists
and spectators start to pull down the paper
that covers everything, but underneath
silver paper appears, making a mirror,
as if, inside, the walls were full of faces.
Rico and *la* Zaira got scared when they saw themselves
but then they laughed, and she remembered
the time that she saw herself in the fountain,
and Rico, to annoy her, threw in a stone, and her face
was broken in the water.
That very Monday morning, Rico asked her
if she wanted to marry him.

8

The next morning by the river, they met a bunch
of people: two hunters, a butcher who was looking
for a rock on which he could sharpen his knives, and a girl
sitting on top of a mound of sand with her legs apart
where you could see everything, so as to entice someone.
In order to not bother her, Rico and *la* Zaira
sat a little ways off, and, in fact,
a truck arrived, kicking up a cloud of dust.
A young man got out of it and in a flash
he had pulled her skirt from her and had pulled off his pants.
La Zaira, who was ashamed,
started to move toward the reeds:
the first time those two made love
was not on their wedding day
because he had to take his father's milk-cow,
who was in love, to the bull at the stud farm
called Bishops' Three Lands. And two days later
they met each other in the countryside when the sunlight
was settling around the haystacks and in the oat fields
which seemed like clear silk, their stalks
swinging in the wind. Rico was so exhausted
that he went to sleep with his mouth open
without being able to taste the cake.

9

They faced the mouth of a hut
entirely covered with plastic, where in August
the *contadini* had cultivated tomatoes
that climbed on stalks. There was a banquet table
twenty meters long, a board laid on wooden sawhorses,
and on top of it, dirty dishes, flasks,
bottles, upright and overturned,
crumbs of bread, forks and spoons,
paper napkins, greasy and crumpled,
and at the back was a man with a hat on his head
and accordion across his shoulders, and he was
fooling around with the keys. He was the musician
who had played for the wedding; the people
had eaten and drunk and then gone away.
Rico and *la* Zaira asked if there was a drop
of water to drink because they were as thirsty as the devil.
They sat down and since there was still all that leftover
    food,
they ate two chicken thighs with that meat
that came off the bone because they were from hens
fed with fodder in those henhouses that look like
    upside-down towers.
A spread this big
Rico and *la* Zaira had seen after the war
when Prince Guidi arrived in Petrella from Rome,
the last of forty generations,
accompanied by a Russian lady who always said: '*Da.*'
He had left money for the bridge and asked that the
    women
prepare snails with the aroma
of wild fennel. *La* Zaira had made the sauce

and even now Rico reminded her that it had been a little
    bit salty.
She got mad and took off, her nose out-of-joint,
and meanwhile the musician played a waltz.
Rico followed her along the river, at any rate, they walked
her in front and him in back so that he said to her
    'Mo du vét?'
'Where are you going?'
She stopped a little ways from a carter
who carried that kind of gravel you find in gardens,
along paths and around flower beds. Rico
arrived short of breath and he did not say one word.

10

The carter invited them into his cart
to carry them to the sea. He was the last
carter of the river and he cared only about his horse.
Where the current had made bigger pools of water
was filled with seagulls that came up from the sea
with fish dead from poison of every type.
The carter let them out
when they were two steps from the water
but there was a fog that covered everything,
a great cloud of dust, of filthy air that seemed like
    a sackcloth
in front of their eyes, and Rico and *la* Zaira
moved forward to approach the sea
which roared in their ears
as if there were a cloud of bees.
But then they got lost in the fog and, screaming and
    calling out,
they did not find each other again, and meanwhile
they were already in the water
up to their ankles. Reaching and reaching
with hands groping in front of their faces,
they touched each other by accident and they embraced
like two who find each other after twenty years in
    America.
Slowly, slowly they started to sit down
in the dry sand, and they stared
into the fog which was lifting
and Rico told her to be patient,
that from one moment to the next, the sea would arrive.

Part Two

The Book of Abandoned Churches

I dedicate these stories to the peasants
who did not abandon the land
in order to refill our eyes with the flowers of spring.

La Vala Dal Cisi Biènchi

Agli era dòg al cisi biènchi ch'al spichéva dróinta la vala. Próima u s'è ròt i vóidar mal finèstri, pu tótt al pórti agli è dvénti fròli e i ciód i dindléva tra la chèrna fràida dagli asi crociféssi ch'agli era pini 'd béus.

Al s'è sfàti cl'an ch'l'à piuvéu tótta l'instèda fina a la próima fira 'd utòubar. U s'avdéva l'impalcadéura di ciód ch'i tnéva sò di pézz ad lègn e i féva una ròba trasparénta che paréva una telaragna. T'una zurnèda che e' vént e' féva se séri, l'à tach a vulè véa i ciód e u n è rèst gnénca l'òmbra dal pórti.

Quant che i gazótt i s'è mèss a fè gazàra alà dróinta, l'aria la era pina ad piumini ch'al caléva zò fina e' sulèr cmè s'al caschés dagli èli di anzal ch'i vulèva te sufétt.

E una nòta da sèch al cisi al s'è squaiè ma tèra tótti insén.

Un muntanèr che sta sòtta Badia l'èlza la mèna drétta se bastòun e u t'insègna zò tla vala di móc ad sas e calzinàz ch'i léus cmè la bèva dal luméghi.

The Valley of White Churches

There were twelve of them, white churches that stood out in the valley. First, the glass of the windows was broken, then all the doors got soft and the nails swayed in the rotten pulp of the crucifix boards, which were full of holes.

They fell apart that year it rained all summer long until the first fair of October. You could see a scaffolding of nails that held together the pieces of wood and made a transparent thing that looked like a spiderweb. One day, when the wind blew for real, the nails flew off and not even a trace of the doors remained.

When the birds started to make a racket there inside, the air was filled with feathers that dropped down to the floor like they had fallen from the wings of angels flying close to the ceiling.

And one night, in one second, the churches, all together, crumbled.

A man from the mountains, a *montanaro*, who lived below Badia, raised his right hand and pointed with his cane down to the valley at the piles of stone and plaster that glistened like the slime of snails.

The Cracks

At Pietra Rubbia, there was a bell that rang without anyone pulling the cord. It was August, and half of Italy came and sat down there, either in chairs they had brought with them, or on a rock, or on the grass.

Every Monday, at exactly eleven o'clock, the clapper started to swing and then it banged against the rim of the bell. The ringing upset the air and the ears. Swallows and sparrows flew like bullets and in the flurry one of them slipped into some of the houses, hitting its head against dressers and walls, and feathers fell on the beds.

The story of the bell that rang by itself lasted a summer, then it didn't ring anymore, not even if you pulled the cord, which was nailed down.

In the meantime, the people from that place went wandering around the world and only the old people remained up there, spending their days looking at the valley that goes down to the sea.

The church is filled with cracks and the door is closed with a padlock. On Sunday, the old people kneel in front of the wall and shout their sins into the fissures so that their voices can make it as far as the altar where there is a spoon, an upside down candlestick and an egg from a hen.

A little boy who lives with his grandfather among all these old people kneels down on Sunday, too, in front of a crack, but right away, he starts to cry because he can't think of a sin. Luckily, his grandfather is there next to him, who whispers and passes him one on loan.

The Black Spot

The charcoal makers had put up a hut that was used as a church. The walls were made of bundles of firewood and on top there were long bundles of sticks that covered the whole thing.

The priest came to say Mass on the feast of the Assumption and almost always people were crowded inside because outside it was raining and the water made all the leaves on the trees sway.

In October of nineteen-fifty, one night, a bolt of lightning hit the church dead on and everything burned.

Now, people from the valley come up here to pray near the black spot of ashes, and when they raise their eyes they see there in front of them, for a moment, that the hut is still standing and the lightning hasn't come.

The Breakfast

Two steps from Sogliano the owner of the shop that sells everything bought a small abandoned church in the woods which he used as a warehouse for toilets to be sold to hotels on the sea.

One Sunday morning, he opens the padlock and closes himself inside to count the piles of toilets which cover the walls and the frescoes that are being eaten by mold.

When he goes to rest after taking inventory, he finds that there near by him on the little steps of the altar is a tray with a cup of something hot and some little pieces of bread with butter.

He looks around with astonished eyes because that very morning he hadn't had breakfast. 'So I came in by myself and I closed myself in with the bolt. And so then, who was here?' From that day his head is filled with thoughts he hadn't had before.

The Words Inside a Stone

Under the floor of the Rectory of the Rosary they found some dead people who were sitting down. They still had socks on their feet of all different colors like they used to make at one time from unraveled sweaters.

From a hole in the foundation some kind of stone fell out, which was not really a stone, it seemed to him. Later, he understood it was a written book, maybe a notebook, which had fancy stitching of string on one side.

A Dutch professor looked at it and looked at it, and discovered that it was the diary of a holy man who had been buried in the church but they had robbed even his bones. One year later, this professor arrived with a huge lens, thicker than the bottom of a bottle even, and he read something inside the stone. Before all those other words were these: More alone than God, there is no one.

The Sandals

Vincenzo was a monk who lived in the mountains inside a cave and he didn't know how to read or write. He kept a lantern lit which had blackened all the walls. With the point of a nail, he lined up stones under the black patina, making little white crosses which stood out against all that soot.

He told those who came looking for him that God is that thing which lets you stand upright. Then he kissed two or three dry leaves that he kept in his pocket and burned them; if, instead, it was a sick animal, then he gave out some fava beans that he kept in a frying pan. He drank rain water which he collected in jars that sat outside the door with open mouths waiting for it to rain.

When his poor dead mother brought him a sweater for his health, he kept his eyes closed for two days, not looking her in the face, and with one arm raised against the ceiling he made a sign that said he paid attention only to the one above.

One summer they saw he was walking barefoot up on top of the mountain and that his sandals were still inside the cave waiting.

Two Coffee Mills

There was a church below Montetiffi, actually two, that were so small they looked like coffee mills; they were right next to each other, about one step apart, with no doors or windows, and inside there were niches where people lit small candles as thin as two matches put together.

Everyone asked for grace and there was an old woman who was always around there with her pig, and she lit a candle every week.

One time they heard her talking directly to St. Nina. 'Listen here,' she said, 'make sure that I die before all the young people in town.' And that day, right after, she died while bending over to pick a leaf of lettuce.

The Sheep

The convent is down below a dirt road covered with holes made by the hoofs of sheep that sink down into the mud in May. The last monk died on his feet leaning against a column.

For a year now, a shepherd has been renting it and in the summer he sits there on the edge of the well in the middle of the courtyard and uses a long cane to tap the sheep that eat the grass around the convent.

The owner is a rich man from Piacenza: every August he comes up for the fresh mountain air and sits under the portico and drinks beer from a bottle with his eyes closed while he lies on a cot. Every so often he and the shepherd eye each other, without saying one word, even for an entire day.

When one of the sheep moved away from the grass and walked over to the rich man from Piacenza to be petted, the shepherd shooed him away with his cane, right away, to get him back into the courtyard.

So now the sheep raises his head and doesn't know who to listen to. Then, he goes through a door under the arcade and walks into the church and picks his way through the empty bottles and potatoes that are strewn all over the floor.

First the dog, then the shepherd, and, last, the rich man from Piacenza went in to look for him but the sheep had disappeared.

There are those who say that in the picture of St. Anthony, in the middle of all those animals that surround him, there is also one sheep that at first was not there.

The Streak

Ever since her husband died, Bice has been reduced to talking to a chicken. She gives it a panful of wet bran to eat and she sits on the steps of the door of her house and keeps it company.

Then the chicken goes out and every once in awhile stops in the piazza or wherever it wants. Later, Bice goes and asks some boys if they have seen it pass by. Every morning, they enter the church where there is a picture of a Madonna sitting down, which in nineteen-fourteen had started to cry, when she heard that the First World War had broken out. Then all the women from Rimini and Ravenna came to pray for their husbands and sons who were in danger.

Then, when the war was over, whoever came, came. Water leaked from the ceiling and, Boom, the snow knocked the whole thing down.

This is how the church ended up abandoned and that painting little by little faded from the wall and became dust. The only thing left was a streak in the plaster which was made by the tears that came from the Madonna's eyes back in those days when she cried.

Bice kneeled in front of that crooked line and the chicken crouched right beside her.

The Butterflies

When Tito Balestra and I went to the sea there were mountains of sand and a *contadino* with long underwear and a cigar in his mouth washing a horse.

They said that inside a dale there was a cistern that was as white as a cup of milk, and sometimes you could see it and other times it was buried under the sand that was blown by the wind or by the sea during a storm.

In nineteen hundred it was covered for thirty years and when it reappeared, there was already fascism. The women who sold produce, who with their bare hands turned the dirt upside down looking for potatoes, used the room for silkworm cocoons.

One night a dust storm blew up and buried it again, but there, underneath, they escaped from the cocoons, more than a million butterflies that started batting their wings and their heads against the walls until the cistern lifted itself up, outside the sand and went away from there.

One day in the middle of the day, Tito and I were sitting under the shade of a shirt tied to a pole and we saw that it was floating in the water of the sea.

A Buttonhole of the New Jacket

On certain evenings the houses of Montebotolino fly away and seem like red spots on top of a transparent web. In the winter, if it rains, they remain on their feet in puddles and the water slides over them like they were rocks.

The confessional of the church is a hut made of fir painted red, with woodworms that even eat the nails. I sat myself down to see if the priest was comfortable. It was a Sunday afternoon and a spider was swaying at the end of a thread that came down from a funnel of silk. And I fell asleep.

Then I had a desire to get to know the priest who due to old age had retired from all his responsibilities and lived in the country near the pine forest of Ravenna. I wanted him to tell me which was the last confession in Montebotolino. He was eighty years old and his hands trembled like they were butterflies about to take off.

Without saying first name or last, he told me that one morning at five-his feet wet because he had walked through grass white with frost-an old woman right away came and kneeled down in the confessional.

In a voice that trembled, she told him that the night before a feast day she sewed shut that little buttonhole in the collar of her husband's new jacket so that he couldn't put a flower in it and show off in front of all the other women. And now she was sorry.

The Bowing Candles

With violets in our mouths and discussing the swallows that make nests in the stalls to eat the gnats that fly around the cows, we arrived at a little church where the caretakers were two brothers and a sister.

They opened the door and all over the floor there were candles, big and small, stuck to the ground, and drops of wax. They were all standing there with their heads extinguished and bending toward the altar in devotion because up above there is a round frame which displays one piece of straw.

You have to know that a thousand years ago a Christian soldier returning home from the war to liberate Jerusalem stole a handful of straw from the stall where the Baby Jesus was born. Then he sold them all over Italy together with some guy who had a saint's bone that he had women who wanted to become pregnant touch.

The brothers and sister light all the candles once a week with a long pole with a wick at the end. They look for a little while at the piece of straw, make the sign of the cross, then together blow out all the candles. For two or three days the inside of the church is dirty from the smoke.

The Bell

for Nino Campèna

The church was near a graveyard where a girl named Unichetta was buried. In order to get a look at the bell, which is the oldest in the mountains, there is a bell tower which is a meter-and-a-half high with two sets of peasant's steps, like two wooden ladders. The first one goes up through a hole: after that, the second one takes you up to the top. Nobody knows who made the bell or in what year.

And one day in Santarcangelo a man in his eighties arrived who was exploring words written in books of another time or written in stones. A friend from Pennabilli little by little gave him a hand on the first and second set of stairs until they arrived up top, worn out and covered with dust.

As soon as this professor saw this old bell suspended in the middle of the arcade above the shaft, he embraced it and held it tight for ten minutes as if it were a son who had returned from the war. Then he let go of it, and he and the other man came back down the stairs taking every precaution.

When he was back on the ground, his hands brushed his coat to shake off the dust, and meanwhile, he said that the bell was made by Iacòbus Aretinus in thirteen hundred and sixteen. How he resolved this problem, God knows, because the part of the bell you can see had no date.

We found out the next year. He said that the stuff written on the bronze was on the other side and that he had read one letter at a time with the fingers of his hand. That's why he held it in an embrace, for no other reason.

The Water of the Parish

In Santarcangelo nobody drinks from the well anymore. It was the holy water that was poured on the heads of children to baptize them and the water that wet the hand of whoever dipped it into the holy water font.

And meanwhile the people who lived around here continued to lift and lower their buckets.

Then, a *contadino* pulled out some water for his artichokes until they sealed the well with a metal sheet, and hung a sign on the edge that said: From here below the water of the Pieve looks up.

The Big Church

The Eden Theater, where in winter the old people went in with hand warmers and their eyes popped out at the stories of the elephants, has been closed for ten years.

However every so often the priest shows a documentary about the Big Church before they made it collapse because they needed gravel to make roads and it was still right at the top of a rock that's as high as a mountain.

You see the bell tower with all the pigeons around it and inside you see the windows that give off glints of light in every direction.

My father was lighting a cigar that morning when it blew up in the air making a cloud of dust with chips from the bell that buzzed like wasps and fragments of marble inscribed with the names of two boys killed in the war.

But now on the theater screen the Big Church is still safe and sound, and people slip out content.

The Corner

There is a little mountain church which has been turned inside out, but it never falls down, even though it is in a valley where avalanches come down at breakneck speed.

The stonemason who made it knew all the mountain's mean tricks and put the church crosswise so that when an avalanche comes, it knocks against the corner that faces the mountains. This way, the avalanche divides in two and slides along the sides of the church to die far off.

The walls have resisted so far, but the desire to come up here and glance at the Madonna is buried under the snow.

The Cherry Leaves

for Andreij Tarkovskij

Above Casteldelci there is a church without a roof and in their arms the walls hold a cherry tree that grew from the floor with branches that touch the sky.

In April there are blossoms and the white slides from the trees until it reaches the valley, then comes the fruit and the blackbirds and wild birds eat it; in the meantime, the leaves get red and a few at a time they fall on heads below.

If someone faces these walls and asks for grace and a leaf falls exactly at that moment, it is a sign that there will be a good response from above.

Tarkovskij turned up in November with a big request, but the leaves had already fallen and made a bed where two sheep were sleeping.

The Graveyard of Rusted Crosses

Maioletto is a town which dropped off the face of the earth one night when there was a torrential rain and the mountain broke in two. Half is still standing, and the other, instead, where there were houses, humans and animals is all closed inside crevasses.

Under the big mound that remains, there is a graveyard with crosses spread out all over the grass or leaning against the wall that forms the square.

A young guy and girl were out walking, looking at the blossoming trees, and went into all that silence to try to read what was written on the pieces of iron and tin. Time had eaten away even the dates. The only thing left were the rusted crosses, abandoned by the bones and names.

And they wrote something with a nail on these pieces of iron, as if they were dead there inside.

SSSH!

for Piera Benedetti

The priest at the rectory at Montelabreve had been fine until fifteen days ago. Then, all of a sudden, he threw himself in bed and he died with his head leaning up against the two peacocks painted on his bedroom wall.

Exactly one second before he closed his eyes forever, he looked over to his niece who was sitting there next to him, and he put his index finger up to his lips and, softly, softly, like it was a breeze, he said: sssh! ; at any rate he said to be quiet. Quiet about what? Was he already hearing voices? Maybe the music that comes from above? Or he didn't want word going around that he had died? Or, if not, some advice to be quiet in general in life? Or was he telling himself to be quiet for fear that his words would come undone in his mouth?

From that day, his niece has understood that she should not talk about these things with anyone. And every so often she goes back in to see the two blue peacocks that have disappeared from the wall.

The White Horse

I was walking around with filthy thoughts in my head that a dream had left in my brain. It seemed there was a naked Madonna tied underneath the stomach of a white stud horse, and I saw her everywhere, even if I put my eyes in the water of the Marecchia which glistened so clean on the stones that it seemed like it wasn't there.

Later, after my head was cleaned out, I walked along a path of sand that took me to the edge of acacia trees whose leaves were completely still and took the sun; but all of a sudden there was one that detached itself from a branch, let's say right here, and then right away one hundred other ones fell down, down to the ground.

And then, they all stopped falling as if by magic. It wasn't because there was a gust of wind that passed by, there wasn't; maybe it was the old leaves that wanted to die all together.

When I arrived at the chapel of St. Veronica, I saw that it had become a stall for a horse. And it was white, the same as the one I had dreamt about. And so? And so, I got out of there.

The Disobedient Hen

They have carried away even the dead at Caioletto and all that is left are holes full of water. There is no one living anymore in the houses.

Inside the church, which is buried underneath walnut-trees, there is a papier-maché statue of St. Anthony among spades and bales of hay piled into stairs. At one time, there was a big feast day and the oxen carried it in a procession among the people who put, at his feet, chickens, pigeons and rabbits, which had to stay for one night on top of the cart closed inside the church.

And a guard behind the altar checked to see if any animals had abandoned St. Anthony's skirt and hopped down.

One night, a hen started to walk around inside the church and in the morning the guard cursed her in front of everyone.

And the priest, who gave back the blessed animals that were going to live to old age because they brought good luck, was left with this disobedient hen that nobody wanted.

It started to get dark and the balloons deflated above the heads of the children, and the priest gave the hen to some poor guy who put it under his arm and went off to eat it right away.

When October came, St. Anthony listened and heard that the walnuts fell on the tiles of the roof of the church and cracked and split apart.

In the night, the wild animals arrived and they ate all of the walnuts, and then rubbed their backs against the walls to say hello to him.

The Garden of the Nuns

The convent of the nuns who had taken a vow not to see anyone in the world anymore, in nineteen hundred, after a landslide, was filled with cracks and little by little the whole thing fell down.

There is nothing left on top of the hill and even the nails have disappeared. In the grass, you can barely see the red strips of brick that mark the foundation.

But the garden which was closed inside walls before was saved, the garden where they took little strolls to get some fresh air and enjoyed looking at the behinds of bees hanging above the flowers' mouths or the wings of butterflies that trembled above the daisies.

The hedges with green leaves and here and there stems of roses, the tureens with geraniums, the broom bush, the lilac tree and all the wild flowers are still alive and there is no grass growing on the gravel paths.

One day, the director of a country band arrived and he realized that the swallows, which were absolutely still on threads of light that passed above the abandoned garden, looked like music written in the sky. And he started singing what he was reading and it was holy stuff.

Now, hardly anybody comes to see the garden and there are evenings you can hear the leaves breathing.

The Mulberry

Carminàz bent mulberry branches until they turned into big shade umbrellas for the women who sewed the hems of sheets. They were clouds of white stuff that they moved with their hands and their eyes pierced the cloth before the needles.

Sometimes it was so hot that the butterflies got sunburned and a girl didn't care if she spread her legs and showed the line where her underpants ended.

Down into this valley of wild grass, which from above Verucchio goes down and meets the water of the Marecchia, would roll the sounds of the bells in San Marino. And right down there, Carminàz made the top of the mulberry-tree into delicate needlework, light as a spiderweb, and, a monk came there underneath to say the evening rosary in May with the *contadini* who cut the reeds.

The light from a huge moon fell on the mulberry and flecks of light passed through the needlework to light the faces of the people who were singing.

The Trench

Every year snow falls in the trench where the charcoal makers put logs in the mud in order to get over to the little cell built at the spot where St. Francis stopped to warm his hands. And in fact, it is called the Cell of the Frozen Hands.

But one night the swollen stream dragged it all away; walls and candles rolled all the way to the sea.

The charcoal makers say that the belltower was left standing so they could hear it on the big feast day.

Now that they are in their beds giving old age a rest, when the bell rings, they get up and go down into the trench.

Translator's Note

If Tonino Guerra is known to English-language speakers, more than likely he is known as a screenwriter who has collaborated with many of Italy's most important postwar filmmakers. And if he is known for his work as a screenwriter, more than likely he is known for his collaboration with Federico Fellini on *Amarcord*. Guerra's touch is everywhere in this film: from the opening scene in which dandelion wisps float and swirl intoxicatingly in the air to the magnificent unfurling of a peacock's tail against a backdrop of snow, to the film's final scene where a wedding party, gathered at a long table underneath a canopy, disbands.

These are some of Guerra's trademarks: the ephemeral, the yearning, and the appearance and disappearance of visions and matter. These trademarks are infused in his prose and poetry, as well as in his screenwriting. But, if Guerra is a conjurer who imagines marvels, they are marvels that coexist with the harshness that is a peasant's resistance and sardonic humor. In Guerra's poetry, as in his screenplays, weightlessness and weight exist together, and the reader does not know from one moment to another whether to expect a lifting up and a floating away, or a plummet, like the sinker on a line as it drops into deep water.

Natalia Ginzburg wrote of Guerra's poetry: 'Loud and solitary, his voice says goodbye to a world which has disappeared.' This past in Guerra's poetry, the Italy he writes of, is emphatically not many things. It is not Gucci handbags and Fendi: belts, or bottles of olive oil and balsamic vinegar in the window displays of upscale American department stores; it is not an espresso bar or a rented farmhouse in Tuscany with central heat. It is not, in short, Italy as consumer product; it is not the Italy that is eternally popular.

It is not a world a tourist sees, but it may be one that he or she carries inside, and even if it is not this very world, it is, perhaps, quite similar to it: a past, perhaps recent, perhaps remote, in which the forest, the sky and the outside world are threatening, a world whose vocabulary is built around the objects of a harsh agrarian landscape. It is a world whose language marks one as different from the educated people of distant cities. It is a language of difficult lives, of privation, in which Death cannot be relegated to certain institutions and communities because it is ever-present and constant and relentless. It is a world in which there has not yet been, in the words of scholar Carlo Ginzburg, 'a victory of written over oral culture,' the first, an extension of the body, the second a thing of the mind.

Why the translation? Why the translation of these particular works? I am not sure, except to say the translations began with recognizing in them things I had seen before. (How, in *Il viaggio*, Zaira pulls a cigar from the mouth of her sleeping husband so he does not get burned; how she twists the loose wedding band around her finger.) It began with the recognition of things I vaguely remembered being told. (How the mountaineers, *i montanari,* died of malaria after finding work in the plains to drain the swamps of the Maremma.) In these poems, I found things. Things? Lost things. Things I was not conscious of having lost, things I did not necessarily miss, but when I found these things, stumbled upon them, brushed against them, had them hurled from the pages at me, I recognized them immediately. They were fragments from somewhere far away, in memory, something like the aroma of rosemary, a smell so powerful, as Guerra writes in *Il viaggio*, it hits you from behind.

In Tonino Guerra's work, there exists the possibility that a marvel can occur, that there can be a transformation of the physical world. This world is compelling: Butterflies descend and cover a town like a blanket of flour. Pages of books that are set on a roof to dry suddenly begin to murmur in the wind. The tracks of an animal in snow mysteriously cease, giving the appearance that a creature with paws has taken flight.

But beauty and tenderness are precarious things, and the space between these marvels and destruction is quite close. The threat of natural elements and economic realities remind the reader that this world can never be mistaken for a pastoral idyll, and this world in Guerra's poems is as repelling as it is compelling: The gruff, cruel love of one brother for another in *The Honey*; the servile deference of Isolina in *The Hut*. It is a coarse world, a fierce world where towns disappear in landslides, and the remaining towns are depleted of young people, who have all left. In a world where loss is the norm, affection is a luxury, and biting humor is one of the few reprieves. In *The Honey,* for example, there is the grim consolation offered by Pinèla the peasant, when he speaks to the narrator who is facing death:

> He said to me: 'Why afraid? Death's not so bad,
> it only comes once.

Integral to Guerra's work is a strong sense of the social and economic realities of this century, including the devastation of rural communities by emigration. Abandoned places haunt the countryside: houses and churches, courtyards and fields. In *The Honey*, there is the pink house where no one lives in front of a field where the horse fair was once held. *The Hut* is a poem built around the image of a hut which has been abandoned and revisited. In *The Journey*, Rico and Zaira come across an abandoned mill and leave behind a *lavadeur*, the fountain in town where women once did the wash. *The Book of Abandoned Churches* is a mediation upon twelve tiny, crumbling mountain churches of stone.

The experiences of both World Wars and the years of fascist rule are interwoven into these poems, and the language echoes with the resiliency and irreverence of survivors who have resisted authority. The poems also reflect the ecological devastation that arrived hand in hand with Italy's economic emergence since World War II, culminating in the final scene of *Il viaggio* in which Rico and Zaira encounter a filthy seashore.

Tonino Guerra's poetry is written, not *in lingua*, that is, in the Tuscan-Italian of standard Italian, but in the dialect of his native Santarcangelo, a town in the Apennine mountains of Romagna. Someone asked me once to read one of the poems in dialect. I said that I could not. Not really. And if I can read them in dialect, it is only because I have learned to. This is the paradox. If I had known how to read them, if I had known all the words, I might not have felt the need to translate them.

At the beginning, it was specific words which prompted me to start the translation, a recognition of some words, an ignorance of others. I perceived this language in fragments, remnants of a cultural heritage. Instead of the standard Italian *dentro*, which means 'inside', was printed *dróinta*, a word which is pronounced with an almost closed mouth, and I pounced on it as a word I knew. I read *gnénca*, a word that is guttural in dialect, whereas *in lingua* there would have been the word *nemmeno*, which means 'not even as much as.' Instead of, at the start of *Il viaggio*, the word *rimandato* ('put off'), there were the words *ch'i éva armànd*.

The language of Guerra's poetry is one in which syllables are dropped, recombined and fused together: the word for Sunday, *domenica,* becomes *dmenga*; the word for tomorrow, *domani,* becomes *adman*. The dialect of Guerra's Santarcangelo di Romagna, in the eastern part of this region near the Adriatic, is not the same as those of my grandparents, which was a language formed in the rugged mountains at the intersection of Modena, Tuscany and Bologna; but it is similar enough for me to hear my grandmother speaking to one of her own.

It is customary for translators to make an apologia for their translation, for all that is lost in the translation, and I likewise make mine. In the case of these poems, there is loss going from the dialect into standard Italian, let alone into English. Words and jokes have been dropped completely because they cannot be translated. For example, in *Il miele,* the name of the character is altered from Pirìn dagli Evi to Pierino delle Api in Italian, which in English means Pirìn of the Bee or Pirìn who keeps bees, in which the label becomes part of the name. Or, in another example, in *The Hut*, Omero warms his bed with a bed warmer, which is called *scaldaletto* in Italian; but in Omero's language a bed warmer is *e' prit* (*il prete*), the 'priest', reflective of the peasants' irreverence toward the clergy, typical of that generation and that culture. This contraption, a metal box which lies between the sheets, couples with a smaller contraption called, naturally enough, the 'nun.'

The sounds of the words in dialect have often been lost, as well. In *The Honey*, after the flood, the monk Sajat-Novà places the holy books onto the roof to dry.

He waits for a month before the books start to show some sign of life. Finally when the wind blows, the pages rustle and he weeps to hear the books talking. In the dialect, the rustling and fluttering pages are captured with the repeated sound of 'z', which is absent in both the Italian and English languages: *al zuclé lizìri ma la brezza de vént* ('a frusciare leggere nella brezza del vento' ('the pages started to rustle slightly in the breeze'). And what cannot be translated, of course, are the most elemental syllables, that baby boy is called a *burdèl*, that mommy is *ma* and daddy is *ba*.

I had to ask myself: Is this translation nothing more than an attempt to recover and put back together fragments left by the trauma of immigration, as if somehow to 'make it better', validate it, acknowledge all the pain over the years caused by the departure and the impossibility of return? Is it an attempt to heal rifts left by the trauma of the separation? And the echoes of these traumas that continue generations later? Of course, that I am writing of it merely re-emphasizes that I am not one of them, neither one who stayed, nor one who emigrated from it. This activity of reassembling fragments to make a whole would be judged by them, I fear, as an extravagant waste of time. The *montanaro*-turned-immigrant-turned-laborer would say: 'You're spending all this time? For what?' They would say: 'The past is done, let it be' — in the same way Guerra's narrator says in *Il miele*:

> I burned all the pages of the books, the calendars,
> the geography maps. For me, America
> is no more, Australia nothing,
> China is an odor in my head,
> Russia, a white spiderweb,
> Africa, a glass of water that I dreamed about.

Is this translation, then, nothing more than an attempt of the good daughter to keep it alive, to put it back together so her own child might be able to recognize something of himself in it? To foster in him compassion and tolerance? Or is it a far less altruistic motivation? A kind of peace offering, a penance, another final attempt to pay off the debt? A grand gesture to say to them again: 'I understand, I see, I know, I honor, I stand in awe of your strength and suffering, now let me have my life, please.' To enter into this world is to be reminded again and again of Filomena in *The Hut* :

> The night before she died, she said
> to all her people who were there around her:
> 'Remember that after us
> there won't be any *us* anymore.'
> It is a kind of burden and blessing you want to be
> free of but of course you cannot.

I now remember now being nineteen years old, at college, on foreign-film night sponsored by the film club, and seeing a Fellini movie advertised. I remember that I was embarrassed because I didn't know what the title meant and felt that I should have. I remember being intimidated because film-going was an activity, I thought at the time, reserved for others who were more culturally sophisticated. I did not recognize in the title a word I had heard all my life, a thousand times, not being able to comprehend this word written, not being able to associate it with those mountain voices which were saying nothing more than *Amarcord. Mi ricordo.* I remember.

Adria Bernardi

About the Author

Born in 1920, screenwriter Tonino Guerra has collaborated with many of Italy's most important filmmakers, including Federico Fellini on films such as *Amarcord* and *E la nave va*, and with Michelangelo Antonioni on films including *Blow Up* and *L'avventura*. He has written more than fifteen volumes of poetry and fiction. His poetry is written in the dialect of his native Santarcangelo di Romagna in the province of Forlì. Guerra's poem *Il viaggio* (1986) was made into a film by Ottavio Fabbri. His work of fiction *I guardatori della luna* (1981) was a finalist for the Premio Campiello.